VOLUME III

CHRISTMAS
WITH
Victoria
VOLUME III

Oxmoor
House.

HEARST COMMUNICATIONS, INC.

Christmas with *Victoria*™ Volume III
©1999 Hearst Communications, Inc., and
Oxmoor House, Inc.

Victoria is a trademark of Hearst Communications, Inc.
Oxmoor House, Inc.
Book Division of Southern Progress Corporation
P.O. Box 2463, Birmingham, AL 35201

Library of Congress Catalog Card Number: 98-65704
ISBN: 0-8487-1883-6
ISSN: 1093-7633
Printed in the United States of America
First Printing 1999

WE'RE HERE FOR YOU!

We at Oxmoor House are dedicated to serving
you with reliable information that expands your
imagination and enriches your life. We welcome
your comments and suggestions. Please write us at:

> Oxmoor House, Inc.
> Editor, **Christmas with *Victoria***
> 2100 Lakeshore Drive
> Birmingham, AL 35209

To order additional publications, call (205) 877-6560.

Victoria
Editor-in-Chief: Nancy Lindemeyer
Art Director: Susan Maher
Field Editor: Ann Levine

Oxmoor House, Inc.
Editor-in-Chief: Nancy Fitzpatrick Wyatt
Senior Editor, Copy and Homes: Olivia Kindig Wells
Senior Foods Editor: Susan Payne Stabler
Art Director: James Boone

Christmas with *Victoria* Volume III
Editor: Adrienne S. Davis
Associate Art Director: Cynthia R. Cooper
Copy Editors: Jacqueline Giovanelli, L. Amanda Owens,
      Catherine Ritter Scholl
Editorial Assistant: Rebecca Flint
Senior Photographers: Jim Bathie, John O'Hagan
Senior Photo Stylist: Kay E. Clarke
Photo Stylist: Linda Baltzell Wright
Assistant Photo Stylist: Jan Gautro
Publishing Systems Administrator: Rick Tucker
Director, Production and Distribution: Phillip Lee
Associate Production Manager: Theresa L. Beste
Production Assistant: Faye Porter Bonner

Contributors
Designer: Rita A. Yerby
Writer: Virginia Gilbert Loftin
Foods Editor: Lisa Hooper Talley

Contents

FOREWORD

*I*t is with great pleasure that we present Christmas with Victoria Volume III,

our third annual collection of inspirations for holiday decorations, gifts, entertaining,

and menu planning. On these pages, you will find new and imaginative ways to mark this

most anticipated season. And tips and instructions will help you perfectly re-create each idea,

adapted to your personal style.

Join us as we visit charming shops and country inns, where the Christmas spirit flourishes.

Delight in the beautiful color photographs that illustrate merry arrangements to fill every

corner of your house, thoughtful gifts for everyone on your list, and unforgettable recipes for

celebrations, large and small. Then return with us to the heart of it all—home—as we inspire

you to welcome guests with innovative adaptations of cherished traditions.

However your holiday unfolds—whether shared with a large, extended family or with

a small circle of loved ones—we wish you a glorious season of laughter and good cheer.

From the Victoria family to you and yours, may your Christmas be merry and

your heart be glad all through the year.

The Editors of Christmas with Victoria

CHRISTMAS ACROSS THE LAND

Come along on a visit to three places with special holiday magic: a Creole inn, a retreat in the Tennessee mountains, and a welcoming home in St. Louis. Let their traditions inspire your own holiday celebration.

TANTE HUPPÉ INN

The home of Suzette Prudhomme Lafon LeComte Huppé has welcomed visitors to Louisiana's Creole country for more than 150 years. The first guests were members of her extended family, who stayed with Tante Huppé during visits to town from their nearby Cane River plantations. Today, Bobby DeBlieux—a descendant of that extended family and the innkeeper of Tante Huppé Inn—delights in confiding that

A poached pear (see recipe on page 129) in an antique sherbet glass presents an elegant beginning to a traditional Creole Christmas breakfast at Tante Huppé Inn.

nearly all the furnishings and the decorative arts in the inn are heirlooms from the 1850s. In fact, most of the library's holdings—atlases, steamboat schedules, and French newspapers—are original to the house, perhaps read by DeBlieux ancestors.

At Christmastime, Tante Huppé Inn blooms with lush native greenery that fills antique vases on the mantel and the sideboard. Following Creole Christmas tradition, guests are offered a Louisiana-style candlelit breakfast, customarily served after midnight on Christmas Eve or on Christmas morning. The four-course menu includes favorite family recipes and ends with a toast of champagne and pecan pralines.

The dining room sideboard (left), overflowing with seasonal greenery, twinkling ornaments, and glowing candles, beckons guests to a formal celebration. With a Christmas favor at each seat, the table (above) is set with plates that offer Creole Scrambled Eggs, Crawfish and Grits, and Tante Huppé's Meat Pies.

BLACKBERRY FARM

When Christmas comes to the East Tennessee mountains, it surely makes its home at Blackberry Farm. Woodsmoke perfumes the winter air at this country house hotel, where the warm seasonal splendor of each room and the unforgettable feasts by Chef John Fleer draw guests to this relaxing retreat.

Dried miniature roses and garlands of greenery from the nearby hills are the holiday signatures in every room of the inn and the farmhouse of its owners, Kreis and Sandy Beall.

Guests share Christmas memories around uniquely decorated evergreens situated throughout the inn. Antique toys encircle a tree in the living room, where gold ribbon entwines the rose-laden branches. Trout fishing in nearby Hesse Creek—a favorite pastime—inspires another Christmas tree's decor of angler trinkets.

Garlands of boxwood (opposite), accented with pinecones, pomegranates, tiny gilded artichokes, and hydrangea, frame broad interior doorways. Every window at Blackberry Farm (right) displays a festive holiday wreath—more than one hundred in all.

Gold ribbon and roses appear in every corner of Blackberry Farm. Guests can enjoy a breathtaking Christmas tree (opposite), crowned with clusters of miniature roses, along with a warm hearth (right), framed with luxurious boxwood swags. On the sideboard (above), a Tennessee mountain feast awaits: country ham, cranberry relish, turnip greens, and, if the fishermen were lucky, rainbow trout cakes.

AT HOME WITH SUZY GROTE

Each Christmas Eve, Suzy Grote opens her St. Louis home to her entire family, as well as to dear friends who are unable to celebrate with their own families.

Suzy's comfortable 1920s-era home is filled with unique furniture and accessories passed down from family or collected throughout her career in interior design and historic preservation.

At Christmas, the house displays a special charm, with a mix-and-match approach born of Suzy's love for antiques and innate sense of what works well together. Decorations are natural, simple, and usually gathered from her yard, such as cuttings of holly and blue spruce placed in antique pitchers or tied into swags to hang above windows, inside and out.

For the Christmas Eve feast, Suzy serves a traditional menu on her favorite antique china pieces. A gingerbread house graces the sideboard, and each guest receives an English cracker that holds a whimsical little gift.

But Suzy is quick to note that gift-giving has become insignificant to her family. For the Grotes and their ever-widening circle of loved ones, sharing time at the table is the best present of all.

Needlepoint stockings from Suzy's extensive collection dangle from the mantel in her red-walled library, a popular place to gather. Stockings hang throughout the house: elegant velvets, knitted heirlooms, all cheerful and lovely, whether displayed singly or as a group.

Twinkling evergreen topiaries and wreaths with pears, quail feathers, and bells made from terra-cotta pots frame the front door (above). Christmas Eve dinner includes curried fruit (right), offered in blue-and-white china. In the library, a miniature tree (opposite) makes its annual appearance on the coffee table to display Suzy's treasure of ceramic gingerbread ornaments.

DECORATIONS

*D*ress the house for Christmas—indoors and out—with fresh fruits, fragrant flowers, festive wreaths, gilded candles, and handmade ornaments.

FRUITFUL DECORATIONS

With shades, sizes, and shapes as varied as those of flowers, fruits have great appeal at Christmastime as decorative elements. Yellow, red, and bright green fruits resemble holiday ornaments when added to an evergreen garland. Mounds of colorful fruits overflowing from crystal compotes fashion quite a tablescape. And cranberries create a splash of holiday color when used in the bottom of a crystal vase filled with cut flowers.

Sugaring a fruit softens its vibrant color, lending a subtle, pastel touch. Consider using several kinds of fruits in a single arrangement so that the contrasting shapes are displayed to their best advantage.

Sugaring Fruit

You will need a variety of fresh fruits, coarse or superfine sugar, a sealable plastic bag, a small paintbrush, egg whites, and waxed paper.

1. Pour the sugar into the plastic bag and set it aside.

2. Using the small paintbrush, generously cover each piece of fruit with egg white.

3. Place one piece of fruit at a time into the bag of sugar and tightly secure the opening of the bag.

4. Gently shake the bag to coat the fruit with the sugar. When the fruit is completely covered, remove it from the bag and let it dry on the waxed paper.

Attached with wire and florist's picks, clusters of fruits and holly berries bring Christmas cheer to an ordinary evergreen wreath (above). Orange and red fruits in a range of sizes and textures are accented with elegant velvet ribbon loops (opposite). Sprigs of heather are tucked between the fruits to fill spaces and to add textural interest.

The French raised the fruit centerpiece to an art form in the seventeenth century, crafting towers of fresh fruits that were often "glued" together with warm caramel.

Such grand arrangements are now much easier to create and require only a florist's foam base cut in the desired shape, florist's picks, and an abundance of fresh fruits. Timing is important with fruit decorations. Plan so that the fruits will look their best for the most special occasions. Apples, oranges, and pineapples may last for several weeks, but thinner-skinned fruits, such as grapes, will stay pretty for only a few days.

Experiment with combinations of colors and sizes. Begin at the bottom of the centerpiece and work your way toward the top, attaching one row at a time, either in concentric circles or in a spiral pattern. Once you have finished, add greenery for a soft accent: try clippings of pine, heather, boxwood, juniper, or ivy.

Fruit pomanders are the simplest holiday art of all to fashion. Make them by inserting cloves into whole lemons, oranges, and other citrus fruits and then gluing on star anise. Wrapped in loops of organdy ribbon, these fragrant balls will spice up your home for several weeks. For concentrated aroma and appeal, pile several pomanders together in a bowl or in a tureen and dust them with cinnamon to sweeten the scent.

ORNAMENTS

*U*nwrapping ornaments each year can be as exciting as opening presents, for each bauble is as cherished as a gift—such as a tiny angel from a first Christmas or the crystal star that must always go on the tree last.

Handmade ornments tell a family's history and are the most beloved of decorations. Prized are paper chains and snowflakes made by children—now grown—a starfish from a seashore vacation, and hand-crafted ornaments collected on trips to faraway places.

Antique ornaments, sometimes too fragile to risk hanging on the tree, are like treasures. Nestle them in a bowl of greenery, out of harm's way, and then display the bowl on a tabletop.

When it is time to put away all the ornaments for another year, be sure to pack them properly in their original boxes (wrapped in acid-free tissue paper) and to store them away from temperature extremes.

Collections of ornaments—antique, handmade, or brand-new—are effectively displayed in groups (opposite), whether amongst the mantel garland, on the tree, or in a tabletop bowl.

*N*ot all handmade ornaments are rustic looking. Antique silver beads become elegant tree ornaments (right) when strung together and looped onto velvet ribbon hangers. Silk upholstery cord wrapped around foam shapes (below) creates graceful globes. Beaded snowflakes (opposite)—each as unique as those found in nature—are easily crafted from aluminum wire and tiny faceted beads in blue, clear, and white.

WREATHS

Round, oval, or oblong, the wreath is an enduring symbol of holiday hospitality.

A wreath made of even the humblest materials conveys a heartfelt welcome, whether it's hung on the front door or merely propped on a bench or on a windowsill.

Wreaths can be created from an astonishing variety of materials: classic evergreens, of course, as well as leaves, nuts, berries, fruits, and cut flowers, to list but a few.

An oval wreath of boxwood and green apple berries hangs from the top of a garden gate, secured with a bright red bow made of ribbon suitable for outdoor use. If you wish to attract birds, substitute red berries, such as holly, pyracantha, or nandina.

When choosing materials, consider where your wreath will be displayed. Will it hang in full sunlight or in a shaded spot? Will it be situated on a covered porch or somewhere exposed to the elements? Will it be subjected to a snowy climate or to a warm winter? These factors will influence how long your wreath will last and how often it will require refreshing with new greenery, berries, or fruits.

Generally, to fashion a wreath, you will need a wreath form, plenty of green florist's wire, florist's picks, wire cutters, garden shears, and a glue gun with glue sticks. Straw, florist's foam, wire, and vine wreath forms in all shapes are available at crafts and garden stores. Or if desired, you may design your own wreath form, using a version of the items listed above.

Here, wreaths take three distinct forms. To create the oval wreath (opposite, below right), cut a thin wooden oval base and then cover the base with florist's foam, secured with florist's tape. Gather greenery into generous bunches and wire the stems onto florist's picks. Insert the picks into the foam.

The round wreath (above and opposite, left) begins with a straw wreath form. Cover the form with sheet moss, attached with wire. Glue hazelnuts to cover the form, until little moss peeks through.

For the rectangular or oblong wreath (opposite, center), wire or tape blocks of florist's foam into a rectangular shape. Insert fresh bay-leaf stems directly into the foam. When using naturals, be sure to harvest enough greenery for a lush, full look.

Fragrant bay leaves shape an oblong wreath; in the foreground, an oval boxwood wreath is accented with bright green berries; and hazelnuts cluster on a classic round wreath (opposite). Trimmed with a crisp taffeta bow, the hazelnut wreath adorns a sunny entrance (above).

WINTER WHITE

Even those who live in warm climates can see their dreams of a white Christmas come true with the artful use of winter white decorations for the holiday home.

Crisp like snow, yet soothing and pristine, white—as well as its variations eggshell, cream, silver, and pale gray—offer a romantic palette ideally suited for Christmastime.

A white theme works with most decors. It's best to use a range of whites, mixing and blending shades for depth and interest.

Stark white used alone becomes flat, but when combined with other shades of white and with silver, it enhances the elegant color scheme.

Introduce the look with silver accessories—candlesticks, serving bowls, urns, and trays—polished to a high sheen to reflect light. Fill silver and creamware bowls with ornaments of silver, pearl, or clear glass. Bring out clean white linens for the dining table and the sideboard, adding cream pillar candles in groups of varying heights.

White organdy dresses and lacy bows (opposite) evoke memories of Christmases past. Antique hatboxes and tins (right), wrapped in white and topped with tiny cream roses, rest like fallen snow beneath the tree.

Dress the Christmas tree in snowy white and shimmering silver (opposite), using delicate ornaments and a cascade of sheer organdy ribbon streamers. Frosted and clear Christmas balls with glittering designs fill a silver-leaf bowl (above). Antique lace pieces pressed between sheets of glass (right) appear like snowflakes amid the branches.

Entwine the branches of a stately evergreen with multitudes of miniature white lights and garlands of pearl beads. Place silver and white ornaments alongside clusters of tiny white flowers or tallow berries tied with white organdy ribbons.

Also keep the winter white theme in mind when wrapping Christmas presents, concealing gifts with papers or fabrics in shades of white. Use white-washed antique tins or classic baker's cartons for boxes. Tie them with silver ribbons and then adorn the boxes with dried white flowers or sprigs of ivy for the finest finish.

For the mantel, create evergreen garlands, accented with nosegays of roses in white, cream, and pale pink. Make little rose garlands to drape across the tops of mirrors and picture frames or to form into rings and surround stout pillar candles.

A dainty swag of silk flowers (opposite) pulls back a curtain to reveal a cluster of creamy candles. Edged with pearl beads, a cream wool stocking (above) waits at the mantel, where glowing pillars stand amongst the greenery and the palest of pink roses.

GILDED CANDLES

There is no easier way to bring a group of guests together than to place candles in their midst.

Candles embellished with silver and gold cast an especially shimmering glow as the light reflects off its source. Tall tapers, sturdy pillars, and dainty votives are easily gilded and have a festive impact when grouped on a table or on a silver tray. Choose a mixture of crystal and silver candleholders in different styles for added interest.

Crystal and silver candlesticks in various heights hold tapers gilded with whimsical patterns, such as stars, polka dots, and pinstripes.

Gilding Candles

You will need a variety of candles, a small paintbrush, silver or gold wax gilding compound (available at crafts stores), heavyweight paper, and a craft knife.

1. To paint pinstripes, dashes, or polka dots, simply apply the gilding compound as desired to a candle, using a paintbrush.

2. To create stars or other designs, first make a pattern stencil. Sketch the desired design onto heavyweight paper. Then carefully cut the design from the paper, using a craft knife.

3. Position the stencil as desired on the candle. Fill in the design with the gilding compound, using a paintbrush or your fingertip.

4. Let the paint dry completely before using the candles.

FRESH FLOWER CHRISTMAS

On gray winter days, fill a vase with fresh blooms and bring springlike color into view. Flowers create a celebration on ordinary days, and at Christmastime, they are a must for cheerful holiday settings.

Choosing which flowers to feature often depends on what is available. If the selection is bountiful, let color inspire your choices: vibrant reds and purples, sweet pinks, or sunny yellows and oranges.

Purple anemones nestle amongst a mass of red anemones, roses, and holly berries, offering a vivid burst of color on the sideboard.

Or you may wish to begin by selecting the container and then the flowers; conversely, you can choose the flowers that, in turn, will inspire the choice of a container.

Do not feel limited to the classic vase, for any watertight vessel—such as a teapot, a goblet, an unusual bottle, a watering can, or a compote—can be used to hold flowers. Once you have selected a container, clean it well with a mixture of bleach and water to eliminate any bacteria on the surface and rinse thoroughly.

Flowers should be arranged for maximum impact and conditioned for long life. Before inserting the flowers, add a commercial flower food, which will provide the proper nutrients to keep flowers fresh for several days.

Store flowers in water until you are ready to arrange them. Recut the stems to the desired length while holding them under cool water.

Some flowers need support inside a container to keep them erect and to maintain the arrangement's shape. A floral frog creates a sturdy base for the stems of tall flowers, such as snapdragons and delphinium. If the flowers demand support higher up their stems, form a grid of florist's tape across the opening of the vase to hold the stems in place.

To ensure the arrangement's freshness, pour out the old water from the container every day; refill it with fresh cold water and add commercial flower food. Cloudy water is a sign of bacteria, which will kill flowers. If the water looks unclean, remove the flowers and scrub the vase with a mixture of bleach and water. Recut the stems before returning the flowers to the vase.

Never place fresh flowers near a heat source, such as a fireplace, a sunny window, or even a television, as the heat will speed wilting.

Candlelight luminates cool white blooms in silver vases (opposite). The large arrangement draws its sculptural appeal from combining white roses, tulips, and ranunculus. Roses and greenery in Christmas colors brighten a silver tea service (right).

A holiday tussie-mussie (above, left) is cleverly tucked into the hand of a

carved cherub on this ornate headboard. Pine garlands and fresh red roses featured

in unexpected places, such as in a bedroom (above, right), fill the entire house.

Gold ornaments cluster beneath a lavish display of

freshly cut yellow roses (opposite).

GIFTS

The joy of giving, in part, is finding the perfect present and seeing the beloved recipient's delight. Our search takes us to three fabulous shops we love. And then we bring you even more ideas for everyone on your list.

FREDERICKSBURG HERB FARM

For Fredericksburg Herb Farm owners Bill and Sylvia Varney, herbal creations are an integral part of Christmas, lifting the spirit of the season to heavenly heights.

The joy they find in humble, practical herbs is contagious to visitors at their 14-acre farm in the West Texas Hill Country. The Varneys remodeled an 1880s limestone farmhouse into an old-fashioned apothecary, tearoom, bed-and-breakfast inn, spa, candle shop, and culinary store, from which they dispense an endless variety of remedies, treats, and wisdom.

Bill and Sylvia began their venture in 1985 as newlyweds, when they opened a store on Main Street in historic Fredericksburg, selling old-world toiletries, natural seasonings, vinegars, and small pots of herbs. After moving to the farm in 1991, they started making their own herb products and have expanded their line each year. "Our farm is about renewal," Bill says. "Using herbs in our gift recipes awakens all the senses."

The Varneys (right) share their love of herbs in their newest book, Herbs: Growing & Using the Plants of Romance. *At Christmas, dried herbs are gathered into swags, wrapped into wreaths, and tied into tiny bundles that hang from the rafters of their shop (opposite).*

Herb Garden Potpourri

The Varneys' signature potpourri recipe is based on a mixture of natural essential oils, which gives it a crisp fragrance. Several dried herbs and whole rose petals add lovely color and texture to the blend. To make it, you will need the following:

1 ounce powdered orrisroot
6 drops rosemary essential oil
6 drops lemon essential oil
6 drops lavender essential oil
6 drops orange essential oil

2½ cups dried lemon verbena
1½ cups dried lemon balm
1 cup dried rosemary
1 cup dried lavender
½ cup dried thyme
½ cup dried sage

Dried rose petals
Dried yarrow blossoms
Dried bay leaves

¼ cup cinnamon powder
½ cup lovage root
6 tablespoons grated orange peel

Combine orrisroot and oils in a small bowl; set aside. Combine lemon verbena, lemon balm, rosemary, lavender, thyme, and sage in a large bowl. Add a handful of rose petals and yarrow blossoms. Sprinkle in bay leaves. Add cinnamon, lovage, and orange peel. Stir the orrisroot mixture into the large bowl and cover. Let the mixture stand away from direct light for 5 days, stirring occasionally.

Fredericksburg Herb Farm (opposite) retains the earthbound humility of its history, with original limestone buildings topped by tin roofs. The herb farm's best-selling potpourri (above), rich with citrusy fragrance, scents every room at the farm.

ANNE FONTAINE

A well-known maxim among fashionable French women holds that "One must renounce all but the essential, so the essential may speak." For French designer Anne Fontaine, essential is defined in her twice-yearly collection of white shirts, crafted of exquisite fabrics and focused on the tiniest of details.

"There is a place in every woman's wardrobe for at least one great white shirt," Anne says. But how to choose only one? At her United States flagship store in Soho, shirts hang like rows of pearls, in varying shades of white, cream, and bisque. Unique closures, splendid collars, and elegant cuffs are hallmarks of Anne's designs.

Whatever the fabric—airy cotton, crisp organdy, or cool piqué—and whatever the style, each shirt is packaged with a delightfully personal detail: a tiny packet of rose sachet (below), which recalls the scent from the linen closet of her beloved grandmother.

A meaningful gift for every stylish woman, this Anne Fontaine blouse (opposite) eschews buttons, opting instead for graceful ties. Pristine shades of white and cream are a perfect foil for the details Anne loves to showcase. The results are never fussy, but simply elegant—and always right.

ANGELINA'S TEA PARLOUR

*I*n a white frame cottage near Portland, Oregon, a mother and a daughter have created a place in which tea is a pleasure to be shared. At Angelina's Tea Parlour, owners Marilyn and Angela welcome guests into their charming tearoom, where tables are draped in vintage lace and set with fine china against a background of romantic white.

Restoration of the circa 1875 cottage took most of two years but was well worth the wait. The cozy rooms provide a welcome respite for those wishing to relax and to enjoy one another's good company. Tea is served by reservation at 4 o'clock, with a holiday menu that includes fresh strawberries and cream, scones with champagne jelly, an array of sandwiches, and dainty petits fours for dessert. Only French teas are served, as a tribute to Paris's original Angelina's, one of the oldest tea parlors in France. The ladies of Angelina's also offer Royal Tea at The Benson, Portland's grandest hotel, built in 1912 in the heart of downtown.

On the silver service, tiny ceramic boxes (opposite) hold samples of Angelina's specially blended teas so that guests may choose the variety with the most appealing aroma. In dressed-up packages (right), Angelina's teas make attractive gifts or holiday favors.

GIFT WRAPS AND GREETINGS

A beautifully wrapped present is twice as special. And a thoughtful giver will put as much consideration into the packaging as to the choice of the gift itself.

Richly patterned wrapping papers or fabrics, perhaps in a single color scheme, look especially inviting clustered beneath the tree. Try choosing packaging materials that best suit the gift or the recipient. Whatever the choice of materials, your personal touch will impart a meaning that will not be missed.

Some of the best packages are those that can be used again, such as fabric-covered hatboxes (opposite) that are edged with braided trims. Stack several gift boxes in a tower tied with ribbon for a dramatic presentation.

Personalized Greetings

Handmade cards convey the most heartfelt messages.

• Use seasonal stamps to decorate blank purchased cards and envelopes. Be sure to test the stamped design on a scrap piece of paper first.

• Add cheerful color to a card with holiday ribbons. Glue a bow onto the front of the card or, using a craft knife, make small slits in the card front to weave ribbon through.

• Cut favorite designs or images from wrapping paper or magazines and glue them to the front of a plain card.

• Attach family photos to the front of cards, using decorative photograph corner mounts.

Glittering gold and silver papers along with silk ribbons (opposite) make sophisticated covers for gift boxes. A series of angel cards (above), drawn by artist Neil Di Teresa of Berea, Kentucky, has become collectible art for the lucky recipients. When a bow is not enough, add a cluster of berries and a single fragrant rose (right).

WARM HEARTS AND HANDS

Knitters know a secret that the rest of us have yet to learn: while hands are busy making needles click, the mind has time to dream. And as the stitches take shape, they fashion comforts to be appreciated—a snuggly afghan, a cozy sweater, a pair of woolen gloves, or a warm hat to chase winter chills.

Needlework is a pastime made for winter, when you can tuck yourself away from the frigid outdoors. While our grandmothers may have knitted or crocheted out of necessity, we are fortunate enough to choose our projects for pleasure. We can stitch at our convenience, during idle moments stolen throughout the day.

Novice needle artists may wish to start with a project that requires uncomplicated stitches, for some detailed work demands a degree of expertise. So perhaps begin with a simply designed muffler or afghan and always use quality yarn.

The best teacher of needle-crafts is an experienced needleworker who is willing to share both her time and talent—gifts to last a lifetime.

Knitting is a relaxing hobby, meant to be enjoyed at leisure, perhaps while sitting by the fire (opposite). A crocheted afghan draped over a chair (above) becomes a decorative and functional element, providing beauty, warmth, and comfort on a chilly evening.

Purchased gloves (right) are transformed into a custom gift when embellished with a duplicate-stitch design. The foundations of a needle project—yarn and needles—need not be stored out of sight, for they add textural interest to a tabletop (below). Knitted of fine ecru wool, a collared pullover (opposite) is disguised as a classic cardigan.

GIFTS OF COFFEE

*I*f a coffee-lover is on your gift list, the possibilities for presents are endless, since drinking coffee is both pastime and passion for many. Shops specializing in coffees offer a wide range of gourmet beans and blends, as well as accompaniments to complement the rich, aromatic brew.

For the coffee-drinker who has everything, offer a present of biscotti, those crisp, flavorful cookies made for dipping into a hot cup of java. Select an assortment at a bakery or at a coffeehouse and, as a special treat, include at least one biscotti covered in chocolate.

Consider giving an antique platter (opposite) filled with delights, such as gourmet beans, biscotti, and specialty candies, to the coffee connoisseur.

Coffee-Lover's Gifts

Those who enjoy drinking coffee will appreciate a gift tailored to their favorite pleasure. Below are some ideas.

• *An antique or collectible cup and saucer, holding chocolate-dipped biscotti and tied with velvet ribbon.*

• *A box of delicious mocha- or coffee-flavored candies.*

• *A bag of gourmet coffee beans and chocolate-covered stirring spoons.*

• *An antique or collectible cream-and-sugar set.*

• *A coffee-scented pillar candle. Or a votive candle and a holder filled with coffee beans; the warmth of the candle releases the scent of the beans. Be sure to keep the beans out of the candle flame.*

A GARDEN OF GIFTS

Gardeners appreciate creative gifts from the garden and the woodland. Look beyond the glitter and the tinsel toward the green and the growing to discover a bounty of presents for the nature-lover on your list.

Choose a plain garden pail and fill it with bulbs and gardening tools—perhaps a set of pruning shears, a wooden-handle trowel, and a weeding tool. For an herb- or vegetable-grower, add garden markers or plant stakes. Annual seeds saved from summer's plantings can be prettily packaged in handmade paper or vellum; crease crisply and then tie the packages with raffia and top with a flower or a leaf that indicates the contents.

Imaginative decorations from the garden are welcome gifts as well. Create holiday ornaments with such naturals as dried blooms and sheet moss.

Select a gardening book or a garden journal and wrap it in handmade paper containing rose petals and fern fronds. Decorate packages with nature's treasures, secured with raffia or twine.

A moss-covered ornament accented with freeze-dried dogwood blossoms (opposite) is ready to hang on the tree with a bit of satin ribbon. A miniature rustic watering can (right) is pressed into service as an ornament when filled with dried roses.

Folded into little packages, handmade papers each hold a handful of seeds (opposite). Decorate a gardener's gift with greenery and other forest finds (above) instead of ribbons and bows. Galvanized pails (right) make useful containers for bulbs, seeds, and other garden-related gifts.

LITTLE LUXURIES

A bit of pampering is welcome at any time of year but most especially during the busy holiday season. Refresh and restore winter-worn skin with soothing natural bath salts and cleansers.

Easy to make and to package in a manner suited to the recipient, these bathtime blends make thoughtful presents for friends, colleagues, and teachers—as well as for yourself.

A gift of fragrant bath salts and powders (opposite) is a luxury that is simple to create and a pleasure to receive. Package in glass jars and, to each, add an identifying label with directions for use written on the back.

GARDENIA BATH SALTS

Essential oil scents these revitalizing salts. For longer-lasting fragrance, choose oil-based scents rather than alcohol-based scents.

1 cup Epsom salts

1 cup coarse salt, such as sea salt or kosher salt

Food coloring (optional)

1 to 2 drops gardenia essential oil

1. In a glass bowl, mix the Epsom salts and the coarse salt, stirring well.

2. To color the salts, add 1 to 2 drops of food coloring to the salt mixture and stir well. For a darker color, add more food coloring; for a lighter color, add more salts.

3. To scent the salts, add 1 to 2 drops of the essential oil and stir well.

4. Pour the salts into clean, airtight containers. To use, pour ½ cup of the salts into the bath under running water.

ENGLISH MUSTARD BATH

Mustard baths are thought to relieve stress, muscle soreness, and sleeplessness.

1 cup baking soda

¼ cup mustard powder

2 drops peppermint essential oil

2 drops rosemary essential oil

2 drops eucalyptus essential oil

1. In a glass bowl, mix all the ingredients together, stirring until the esssential oils are evenly distributed into the powder.

2. Pour the mixture into clean, dry containers. Perhaps reuse an empty mustard tin for one container, tying it with a colorful ribbon bow.

3. To use, pour ½ cup of the mixture into the bath under running water. Relax in the bathtub for 15 to 20 minutes. After the bath, rinse in a cool shower.

SCENTED MILK BATH

Fresh milk—high in protein, calcium, and vitamins—is easily absorbed by the skin, leaving it soft and radiant.

2 cups dry powdered milk

1 tablespoon dried orange peel

2 tablespoons dried lavender flowers

½ tablespoon dried rosemary

1. Pour the powdered milk into a large glass bowl.

2. Using a coffee grinder or a food processor, finely grind citrus peel, lavender flowers, and rosemary.

3. Add the ground ingredients to the powdered milk, stirring well.

4. Pour into clean, dry containers. To use, pour ½ cup of the mixture under running water into a warm bath. Soak in the bathtub for 15 to 20 minutes.

VICTORIAN CLEANSER

A gentle nonsoap cleanser, this powder has a refreshing scent and turns a wonderful shade of lavender when wet.

2 tablespoons oatmeal

1 teaspoon dried lavender flowers

1 teaspoon dried red rose petals

2 tablespoons white kaolin clay (available at pharmacies or natural food stores)

1. In a coffee grinder or a food processor, finely grind oatmeal and dried flowers until the mixture resembles bread flour in consistency.

2. Add the white kaolin clay, stirring well.

3. Pour into a clean, dry container. To use, combine approximately 1 teaspoon of powder with water in the palm of your hand, forming a smooth paste. Gently clean your face with the paste and rinse with cool water.

An assortment of beauty products for the bath (above) features facial

cleansing grains, beeswax lip balm, scented French soaps, and linen towels edged

with cut velvet. Place these items in a graceful basket and then include some-

thing especially suited to the recipient, such as a recording by a favorite musician,

a best-selling book, or a framed photograph of a meaningful memory.

BOOKS FOR CHRISTMAS

A classic Christmas book is a treasure for anyone, especially for a child who has yet to hear what is sure to become a beloved story.

Ask a local bookstore owner for help in locating a collectible edition. Or choose a new hardcover volume; inscribe a message to the recipient on the inside cover and include the date.

Begin a cherished tradition by reading from a literary favorite on Christmas Eve.

Christmas classics, such as Dickens's A Christmas Carol (opposite), are timeless gifts. Personalize the book by adding a ribbon-and-charm bookmark or by including a personal message or a favorite quotation.

Beloved Christmas Tales

Enjoy these wonderful Christmas stories year after year.

• A Christmas Carol: *Charles Dickens's well-known story of Ebenezer Scrooge's encounter with the Ghosts of Christmas Past, Present, and Future.*

• A Visit from Saint Nicholas: *Clement Moore's poem, in which jolly old Saint Nick names the eight tiny reindeer.*

• A Child's Christmas in Wales: *Dylan Thomas's endearing holiday fable, based on his own experience.*

• A Christmas Memory: *Truman Capote's memoir of a childhood Christmas in the rural South.*

• The Gift of the Magi: *O. Henry's beloved short story about unselfish love.*

• Little Women: *Louisa May Alcott's novel, in which Christmas comes to four sisters in a most unexpected way.*

I heard the bells on Christmas Day
their old, familiar carols play
and wild and sweet
the words repeat
of peace on eart...

...will to m...
...dswor...

ENTERTAINING

Gracious entertaining combines the loveliest holiday traditions with thoughtful ideas from the host. Here, you'll find inspiration for beautifully presented occasions to be enjoyed by one and all.

CHEESE COURSE

The French have long known that cheese well deserves a course of its own. Paired with a suitable wine and accompanied by small fresh vegetables or fruits, the cheese course is served right before dessert.

A holiday cheeseboard can feature a single whole cheese, such as Mont d'Or or Brie, garnished with cranberry marmalade and served with a crusty bread. The classic French cheese course offers a selection of five to seven cheeses from different families—goat, coated rind, hard, cooked, washed, and veined—and from assorted regions, such as Normandie, Auvergne, and Savoie. Three cheeses from the same region are a perfectly acceptable compromise.

Serve all cheeses at room temperature—so that flavors are at their peak—with traditional breads. Begin with the mildest selection, such as goat or sheep cheese, and always finish with a veined cheese, such as Roquefort or Bleu des Causses. Pair with a wine from the same region as the cheeses.

Present cheeses on plates or platters of glass, marble, wood, or porcelain (opposite). Avoid silver or stainless serving pieces, for they will affect the taste. Grapes, berries, and other small fruits (right) are a fine accompaniment, lending color and texture to the presentation.

TOASTING THE SEASON

A sparkling glass of wine, brandy, or even eau-de-vie raised in salute turns any occasion into a ceremony, especially during the holidays. Toasting special moments with champagne is an undeniable tradition, but there are many other excellent choices: sherry, which recalls all things British; fruit brandies, such as pear, raspberry, grape, or cherry; and dessert wines, such as classic French Sauternes or Italian moscatos.

Vodka laced with raspberries and mint (opposite) offers a colorful alternative to traditional celebratory libations. Stemmed glasses make any beverage more festive. They serve a practical purpose as well, preventing the warmth of the hand from raising the temperature of the wine.

Port Wine

Port, a British favorite actually borrowed from Portugal, is an acquired taste, to be sure.

Rich and strong, port is meant to be slowly sipped and savored, perhaps with a bit of fruit, a handful of nuts, or a wedge of sharp Stilton cheese. Ruby ports are tangy and sweet; tawny ports are paler and gentler. Most ports are aged in wooden barrels for 5 to 10 years, but true vintage ports mature for at least a dozen years, sometimes twice that long.

The best ports offer a peppery, plummy flavor combination. Serve port ever so slightly chilled at the end of the meal, passing the decanter clockwise around the table in the English manner. Tiny port glasses make a classic presentation, but any small claret glass will do.

TABLE GRACES

Traditional formality has yielded to a more relaxed style of entertaining. These days, hosts can create an atmosphere that reflects their particular lifestyle—whimsical or elegant, minimalist or embellished—while upholding the standards of grace and hospitality.

Whether the mood is casual or formal, guests will notice the attention paid to the smallest details: handwritten cards to mark each place, a lovely menu card between place settings, and party favors wrapped in shiny satin ribbons.

Bring out a collection of china saved over the years or acquired through travels and incorporate it into your table decorations and serving plan.

Whatever your personal style, let your inspiration come from the things you love—shared with the people you love—and the results will be divine.

Ribbons on the party favors (opposite) complement the ruby red hues in the hand-painted plates set on an heirloom tablecloth. A fresh leaf becomes a place card (right) and is secured by a cluster of flowers and greenery, gently pressed into the rind of a ripe pear.

Matching the china's holiday theme, a snowy linen napkin (right) is tied with a simple gold cord and a bit of greenery. Hand-lettered menu cards (below) are a lovely keepsake from a memorable meal. Unique holiday table linens (opposite) are created by stamping a winter-pear design in gold on hemstitched napkins, mats, and table runner. Painted gold edges and tiny beads sewn onto the napkin corners provide added interest.

Menu
Mushroom Strudel with Bearnais
Roasted Pheasant with Chestnut Fenn
Poached Pears Filled with Cra

CENTERPIECES

The centerpiece is the focal point of the holiday table. And whether it is tall or small, grand or simple, the decoration must be just right.

The centerpiece complements the celebration and should reflect the mood of the event. It need not sit upon the table itself but may reign over the occasion from the sideboard; this is especially true if the meal is being served buffet style, in which case, the centerpiece can be large and regal. But on the table, it must not interfere with the view from guest to guest, and its greenery should not extend too close to the dishes at each place setting.

Intricate arrangements that take hours to assemble are magnificent but, sometimes, outshine the rest of the presentation. More often, a simply executed centerpiece design works best, for it subtly complements every other effort.

Even with those caveats, centerpieces are a joy to design and to behold. Flowers and fruits and candles, in exquisite containers and imaginative groupings, seem to enhance the food and the company, making a meal more festive.

Stacked ironstone cake stands form the foundation of an impressive centerpiece that incorporates roses, dangling fig, magnolia leaves, and small fruits. Dipped in melted paraffin to preserve them at their peak, the roses can simply be set amid the greenery.

$\mathcal{V}$intage silver cake stands (opposite) take center stage on a round table. Sprigs

of fresh and fragrant sage, thyme, and other herbs are tucked into clusters of tiny cham-

pagne grapes, deep wine-colored roses, baby artichokes, and gilded pears. Similar in

concept but different in scale, varied topiaries of evergreens and berries in coordinating

vases (above, left) form tabletop trees in a casual setting. Cuttings from the winter

garden overflow from a tiny urn for a quick and beautiful centerpiece (above, right).

CHRISTMAS DINNER

When the family gathers at the holiday table, they come to share not only the meal, but the moment as well. So whether you serve a sumptuous feast or a simpler selection of traditional favorites, choose from our menu and revel in the results.

Menu

BEVERAGES: *Choose one or two.*
Vanilla Milk Punch
Champagne Punch
Warm Cranberry Wassail

APPETIZERS: *Choose one or both.*
Sugar-Glazed Nuts
Spinach-Cheese Tartlets

SOUPS: *Choose one.*
Tart Apple and Squash Soup
Wild Mushroom Bisque

ENTRÉES: *Choose one or two.*
Fruit-Stuffed Crown Roast of Pork
Roast Turkey with Porcini Mushroom Dressing
Goose with Gold Rice and Chanterelle Stuffing

SIDE DISHES: *Choose two to four.*
Corn Pudding
Potato Gratin with Gruyère
Braised Red Cabbage, Apples, and Raisins
Crabapple, Ham, and Cornbread Dressing
Julienne Vegetables with Wild Garlic
Sweet Potato Soufflé with Persimmon Glaze and Barbecue Spiced Pecans
Candied Yams and Squash
Cranberry, Pomegranate, and Shallot Relish
Orange-Glazed Brussels Sprouts
Herb-Roasted New Potatoes

BREADS: *Choose one or two.*
Herbed Focaccia
Skillet Cornbread
Sweet Potato Crescent Rolls

DESSERTS: *Choose one or both.*
Deep-Dish Black Plum Pie with Wild Pear Anglaise
Sour Cream-Pumpkin Pie

Vanilla Milk Punch

This creamy punch incorporates brown sugar and brandy flavored with fresh vanilla beans.

1 quart whole milk
½ cup Vanilla Brown Sugar (recipe below)
1 cup Vanilla Brandy (recipe below)
½ cup dark rum
Freshly grated nutmeg

1. In a large saucepan, stir the milk and Vanilla Brown Sugar over medium heat just until the sugar dissolves. Stir in the Vanilla Brandy and rum.
2. Heat through just until warm. Ladle the warm punch into cups. Sprinkle with nutmeg.
    Yield: 6 to 8 servings.

Vanilla-Flavored Sugar

4 cups either granulated sugar, firmly packed dark brown sugar, or confectioners' sugar
1 vanilla bean, split in half lengthwise

1. Fill a 1-quart glass jar with a tight-fitting lid with either granulated, dark brown, or confectioners' sugar. Add the vanilla bean.
2. Seal the jar and store at least 1 week in a cool, dark, and dry place. When sugar in the container is used up, add sugar until the vanilla bean loses its flavor.
3. Stir the granulated sugar into a cappuccino. Use the brown sugar in Vanilla Milk Punch. Sprinkle the confectioners' sugar over fruit.
    Yield: 4 cups.

Vanilla Milk Punch

Vanilla Brandy

1 cup brandy
1 vanilla bean, split in half lengthwise

1. Pour the brandy into a 1-pint glass jar with a tight-fitting lid. Add the vanilla bean. Seal the jar and store at least 1 week in a cool, dark, and dry place.
2. To serve, stir the brandy to taste into yogurt and serve with fresh fruit, drizzle it over a fresh fruit salad, or use it in Vanilla Milk Punch.
    Yield: 1 cup.

Champagne Punch

1 gallon fresh-squeezed orange juice
1 gallon cranberry juice
2 quarts pineapple juice
3 liters ginger ale
2 (750 ml) bottles champagne (sweet or dry varieties)
Orange slices and fresh strawberries for garnish

1. Combine the juices and ginger ale.
2. Gently stir in the champagne just before serving. Add ice and garnish with orange slices and strawberries.
    Yield: 45 (6-ounce) servings.

Warm Cranberry Wassail

2 cups apple cider
2 cups cranberry juice
1 lemon quarter
1 orange quarter
2 tablespoons brown sugar
5 whole cloves
2 whole cardamom pods
2 whole allspice
2 slivers fresh gingerroot
1 (3") cinnamon stick
1 (20-ounce) bottle pale ale (such
    as Bass) (2½ cups)
⅓ cup apple jack brandy or
    regular brandy
⅓ cup spiced rum (such as
    Captain Morgan's)
Cinnamon sticks for garnish

1. In a large nonreactive saucepan, combine the cider and cranberry juice. Squeeze the lemon and orange wedges into the juice mixture, then add the rind portions. Stir in the brown sugar.
2. Tie the cloves, cardamom, allspice, gingerroot, and cinnamon stick in a cheesecloth bag. Add to the juice mixture.
3. Bring to a boil, stirring to dissolve the sugar. Reduce heat and simmer for 20 minutes.
4. Stir in the ale, brandy, and rum. Simmer for 10 minutes.
5. Remove the spice bag and fruit with a slotted spoon. Serve the wassail warm in glasses. (Pour the wassail over the back of a teaspoon set in each glass to prevent breakage.) Garnish with cinnamon sticks.

Yield: 6¼ cups.

Sugar-Glazed Nuts

Sugar-Glazed Nuts

4 egg whites
2 cups sugar
½ cup brut champagne
2 teaspoons salt
8 cups whole nuts
3 teaspoons ground spices

1. Preheat the oven to 250°. Spray 2 (15" x 10" x 2") baking pans with nonstick cooking spray.
2. In a large bowl, whisk the egg whites until lightly beaten. Add the sugar, champagne, and salt. Whisk until blended. Add the nuts and spices of your choice. Stir until coated. Spread the mixture into baking pans.
3. Bake at 250° for 1 to 1¼ hours or until the coating is absorbed and the nuts appear dry, stirring occasionally to prevent sticking.
4. Remove the mixture from the pans at once and cool on waxed paper-lined wire racks, separating the nuts with 2 forks.
5. Store the mixture at room temperature in an airtight container.

Yield: 11 to 12 cups.

Spinach-Cheese Tartlets

Pastry:

1/2 cup cold butter, cut into pieces

1/4 pound chilled lard, cut into pieces

2 1/2 cups all-purpose flour

4 to 6 tablespoons ice water

Filling:

4 large eggs

1 1/2 cups cottage cheese (12 ounces)

2 cloves garlic, minced

1 small onion, finely chopped

1 (10-ounce) package frozen chopped spinach, thawed and well drained (press water out of spinach through a sieve)

1 cup (4 ounces) shredded Monterey Jack cheese

1/2 cup freshly grated Parmesan cheese

1/2 teaspoon salt

Spinach-Cheese Tartlets

To make Pastry:

1. Cut the butter and lard into the flour with a pastry blender until the mixture resembles peas.

2. Sprinkle the ice water over the mixture one tablespoon at a time, stirring with a fork until the pastry is well blended and forms a ball.

3. Flour the dough lightly. Wrap it in plastic wrap and refrigerate for 1 hour.

4. Divide the chilled pastry in half. Working with half of the pastry at a time, roll the pastry out on a floured surface to 1/8". Cut the pastry to fit into tiny tartlet pans. Press the pastry gently into the pans making sure the dough fits into the corners. Press the overhang at the upper edge of the pan to pinch it off. Prick the dough on the bottom with a fork. Place the pans on a baking sheet and place in the freezer until the pastry is firm, for about 15 minutes.

5. Cut small squares of aluminum foil (about 3" x 3"), one sheet for each tartlet.

6. Preheat the oven to 375°. When the dough is frozen, press the aluminum foil, shiny side down, into each piece of the frozen pastry shells. Spoon dried beans into the foil to keep the pastry shells even during baking.

7. Bake for 12 to 15 minutes or until the aluminum foil lifts easily out of the shells. Remove the baking sheet from the oven. Remove the aluminum foil and the beans from shells.

8. Continue baking for 8 to 10 minutes more or until the shells are very lightly browned and firm. Remove the pastry shells from the oven and cool completely in the pans on wire racks for about 45 minutes.

9. To remove the pastry shells from the pans, gently turn the pans over, allowing the shells to fall out. The pastry shells may be stored in an airtight container for a few days at room temperature or frozen for several weeks.

To make Tartlets:

1. Preheat the oven to 375°. Beat the eggs in a small bowl. Add the cottage cheese, garlic, and onion. Mix well.

2. Add the spinach, cheeses, and salt. Stir until well combined.

3. Fill each shell with about 2 tablespoons spinach-cheese filling and place on baking sheets. Bake for 20 to 22 minutes or until the tartlets are puffed and golden. Serve hot.

Yield: 30 to 32 tartlets.

Tart Apple and Squash Soup

Granny Smith apples and acorn squash, classic autumn produce, mingle in this creamy first-course soup.

3 cups chicken stock or broth
1 acorn squash, seeded and coarsely chopped
2 Granny Smith apples, peeled, cored, and chopped
1 small onion, chopped
1 celery stalk, chopped
2 teaspoons minced fresh rosemary
1 (3") cinnamon stick
Salt to taste
1/4 cup fresh bread crumbs
1/4 cup unsalted butter
Salt and freshly ground pepper to taste
Milk or heavy cream, to taste
Freshly grated nutmeg, fresh rosemary sprigs, and vine-ripened cherry tomatoes for garnish

1. In a large saucepan over medium-high heat, bring the stock to a boil. Add the squash, apple, onion, celery, rosemary, cinnamon stick, and salt. Simmer, stirring occasionally, for 20 minutes or until the squash is tender. Discard the cinnamon stick.
2. In a food processor or blender, puree the squash mixture in batches, then strain through a sieve back into the saucepan. Add the bread crumbs and butter. Season with the salt and pepper. Add a little milk or cream if the mixture is too thick.
3. Cook the soup over medium heat, stirring until hot. Garnish with the nutmeg, rosemary, and tomatoes.
Yield: 6 servings.

Wild Mushroom Bisque

12 ounces assorted fresh wild mushrooms, sliced
3 tablespoons minced shallots
3 tablespoons unsalted butter
7 3/4 cups chicken broth, divided
3 tablespoons uncooked long-grain rice
1 tablespoon tomato paste
1 1/2 teaspoons chopped fresh thyme or 1/2 teaspoon dried thyme
Pepper to taste
3/4 cup heavy cream
1/2 cup dry sherry
2 tablespoons finely minced sweet red pepper

1. In a large skillet, sauté the mushrooms and shallots in the butter until tender. Using a slotted spoon, transfer the mushroom mixture to a Dutch oven, reserving the drippings in the skillet. Set the mixture aside.
2. Add 3/4 cup chicken broth to the reserved drippings in the skillet. Bring the mixture to a boil, scraping up any browned bits from the bottom of the skillet. Reduce heat. Cover and simmer for 5 minutes.
3. Add the broth mixture, rice, tomato paste, thyme, and pepper to the mushroom mixture. Mix well. Stir in the remaining 7 cups of broth. Bring to a boil. Reduce heat. Cover and simmer for 1 hour.
4. Strain the mushroom mixture, reserving the vegetables and stock. In a food processor or blender, puree the vegetables with some of the stock in several batches.
5. Combine the pureed vegetables, any remaining stock, cream, sherry, and red pepper in the Dutch oven. Heat gently, stirring occasionally for 20 minutes. Do not boil.
Yield: 6 to 8 servings.

Winter Squashes

Members of the gourd family and natives of the Americas, squashes vary widely in shape, size, and color. Pilgrims thrived on winter squashes since the hard skins prevented the squashes from spoiling fast. Winter squashes include: Butternut—pear-shaped with light-brown skin and yellow flesh. Acorn—a favorite winter squash; best when paired with spices, such as cinnamon and nutmeg. Turban—found in all sizes; actually shaped like a turban. Hubbard—large with knobby, green skin and bright orange flesh.

Tart Apple and Squash Soup

Dried Prunes

Over 200 varieties of plums exist, but only a few are suitable for creating dried prunes. Most dried prunes are produced from French Prunes ("prune" meaning plum in French) which have a very high sugar content that allows them to be dried in the sun without fermenting around the pit. Prune tree orchards are dedicated to growing only plums that produce dried prunes.

Having an ancient heritage, prune trees are thought to originate from Western Asia. These fruit trees were eventually carried westward into South Central and Western Europe where they've thrived for years.

In 1856, prune trees were introduced to North America by Louis Pellier, a French nurseryman who had come to California to search for gold. After finding no gold, Pellier purchased land in California and returned to the nursery business, planting a French prune tree orchard. By the early 1900s, approximately 90,000 acres in California were covered with prune orchards, supplying dried prunes to most of the world.

Fruit-Stuffed Crown Roast of Pork

Each generous serving of this stately entrée reveals a "pocket" filled with dried apricots and prunes.

Stuffed Crown Roast of Pork:
1 (6-pound) crown roast of pork (about 14 ribs)
Dried prunes and dried apricots equal to the number of ribs in the roast
Salt and pepper to taste
1 cup Madeira wine
¼ cup molasses
1 tablespoon dried thyme

Gravy:
⅓ cup all-purpose flour
2 cups beef broth, divided
1 teaspoon dried thyme
Pepper to taste

To make Stuffed Crown Roast of Pork:
1. Preheat the oven to 350°. On the outside of the roast, using a thin sharp knife, make 1" slits between each of the ribs, cutting at a 45° downward angle into the loin meat of each chop to form a deep pocket. The knife blade should extend down to the bottom of the roast.
2. Using a blunt-end knife or small spatula, stuff 1 prune and 1 apricot into each pocket. Place the roast with rib-bone tips up in a shallow roasting pan. Season with salt and pepper.
3. Bake at 350° for 1½ hours or until a meat thermometer inserted into the thickest part of the meat registers at least 130°.
4. In a small bowl, combine the Madeira and molasses. Mix well. Pour the mixture over the roast. Sprinkle with the thyme.
5. Bake for 1 to 1½ hours more or until the thermometer registers 160° to 170°, basting occasionally with the pan juices.
6. Remove the roast from the pan, reserving the juices in the pan. Tent the roast with aluminum foil and let stand for 15 minutes before carving.

To make Gravy:
1. Skim the fat from the pan juices. Measure ¾ cup pan juices back into the roasting pan.
2. In a small bowl, stir together the flour and ⅔ cup broth until smooth. Stir the flour mixture, remaining 1⅓ cups broth, thyme, and pepper into the pan juices.
3. Cook over medium-high heat, stirring constantly, until the gravy thickens and boils.
4. To serve, carve the roast between the ribs to form chops. Serve the chops with the gravy.
Yield: 6 to 8 servings.

Fruit-Stuffed Crown Roast of Pork

Roast Turkey with Porcini Mushroom Dressing

(photograph on page 98)

1 (14-pound) turkey
1 bunch fresh rosemary sprigs
6 large fresh sage leaves
1 cooking apple, cut into quarters
1 stalk celery, cut in half
1 onion, cut in half
$\frac{1}{2}$ cup butter or margarine, melted
Apple wedges, kumquats, fresh
　　rosemary sprigs, fresh sage
　　leaves for garnish

1. Preheat the oven to 350°. Remove the giblets and neck from the turkey; reserve for another use such as making broth. Rinse the turkey with cold water. Pat the turkey dry and drain the body cavity well. Place the turkey in a greased broiler pan or roasting pan. Lift the wingtips up and over the back, and tuck under the bird.
2. Loosen the skin from the turkey breast without totally detaching the skin. Carefully place several rosemary sprigs and sage leaves under the skin. Replace the skin.
3. Place the apple quarters, celery, and onion into the body cavity of the turkey. Place the remaining rosemary and sage leaves into the neck cavity. Brush the entire bird with melted butter. Loosely cover the turkey with heavy-duty aluminum foil.
4. Bake at 325° for $3\frac{1}{2}$ to 4 hours or until a meat thermometer inserted in the meaty part of a thigh registers 180°, basting often with the pan juices. Uncover the turkey during the last hour of cooking. (To prevent overcooking, begin checking the turkey for doneness after $3\frac{1}{2}$ hours.) Remove the turkey from the roasting pan; cover and let stand for 15 minutes before carving. Reserve the pan juices for gravy. Garnish, and serve with Porcini Mushroom Dressing.
　　Yield: 12 servings.

Porcini Mushroom Dressing

Rice:
2 cups uncooked wild rice
$\frac{1}{2}$ cup each diced carrot, celery, and onion
3 cups turkey or chicken stock
$\frac{1}{2}$ cup Chardonnay or other dry white wine
Salt and pepper to taste
2 to 4 tablespoons unsalted butter, or to taste

Mushroom Mixture:
2 to 4 tablespoons unsalted butter
2 to 4 tablespoons extra-virgin olive oil
1 pound porcini mushrooms, cleaned and cut into pieces
3 tablespoons finely chopped garlic
3 tablespoons finely chopped shallots
Salt and pepper to taste

To make Rice:
1. In a medium bowl, combine the rice and enough cold water to cover. Let stand for 1 hour. Drain.
2. In a large saucepan, combine the drained rice, carrot, celery, onion, stock, wine, salt, and pepper. Bring the mixture to a boil. Simmer, covered, for 15 minutes. Cook, uncovered, for 30 minutes or until the rice is tender. Stir in the butter until melted.

To make Mushroom Mixture:
1. In a large skillet, heat the butter and oil over medium-high heat. Add the mushrooms, garlic, and shallots. Cook, stirring occasionally, for 5 to 7 minutes.
2. Add the mushroom mixture to the rice mixture. Stir to combine. Add salt and pepper to taste. Cook over medium-low heat until heated through.
　　Yield: 6 servings.

Goose with Gold Rice and Chanterelle Stuffing

Stuffing:
$\frac{1}{2}$ cup unsalted butter
4 celery stalks, diced
1 large onion, diced
1 sweet red pepper, seeded and diced
1 pound chanterelle mushrooms, sliced
3 cups uncooked Carolina gold rice or long-grain rice, rinsed in three changes of water
1 tablespoon salt, or to taste
$1\frac{1}{2}$ teaspoons cracked pepper
$\frac{1}{4}$ cup chopped fresh sage
1 tablespoon dried lavender
6 cups duck or chicken stock or canned chicken broth
6 large eggs, beaten lightly

Goose:
1 (9- to 12-pound) goose, rinsed and patted dry
$\frac{1}{2}$ lemon
Salt and pepper to taste

To make Stuffing:

1. In a large saucepan over medium heat, melt the butter. Add the celery, onion, and red pepper. Cook, stirring, for 3 minutes. Add the mushrooms and cook, covered, stirring occasionally, for 5 minutes. Add the rice, salt, pepper, sage, and lavender. Cook, stirring, for 1 minute. Add the stock. Bring the mixture to a boil.

2. Reduce heat and simmer over low heat, covered, for 20 minutes or until all the liquid is absorbed. Let cool, transfer to a bowl, and fluff. Do not stuff the goose until ready to cook it. Stir the eggs into the stuffing just before spooning it into the goose.

3. Bake any stuffing that remains in a buttered shallow baking dish. Bake, covered, at 325° for 35 to 40 minutes or until heated through.

To prepare Goose:

1. Prepare a charcoal grill with a spit or build a hearth fire with hot coals and assemble a spit over the coals. Alternatively, preheat the oven to 425°.

2. Rub the inside and outside of the goose with the lemon and season with salt and pepper. Loosely stuff the body and neck cavity with the stuffing, reserving any additional stuffing. Truss the goose.

3. Immediately place the goose on a spit. Place a drip pan under the goose and arrange the coals around the pan. Prick the skin of the goose as it turns on the spit to release the excess fat. Roast the goose for 2¾ to 3½ hours or until a meat thermometer placed in a thigh of the goose registers 180° and in the stuffing registers 165°. (The legs should move easily in the joints when tested.)

Alternatively, place the goose on a rack in a shallow roasting pan, gently prick it around the legs and lower breast with the tip of a small knife, and roast it for 30 to 35 minutes in the preheated 425° oven or until golden. Reduce the oven temperature to 325° and continue to roast the goose for 2½ hours or until a meat thermometer placed in a thigh of the goose registers 180° and in the stuffing registers 165°, pouring off the pan drippings as they accumulate.

4. Place the goose on a cutting board and let stand, loosely covered, for at least 20 minutes before carving.

Yield: 6 to 8 servings.

Mushrooms

Exotic varieties of edible mushrooms have become commonplace in the market. Some mushrooms are as dainty as violets, with ruffled caps and slender stalks. Others take sturdier forms, with broad, spongy heads and thick stems. And most are available dried or fresh, whole or trimmed.

Varieties of edible mushrooms include the following:

- *Cèpe—rich and meaty and ideal for sautéeing.*
- *Chanterelle—unmistakable with its frilly, yellow trumpet-shaped head.*
- *Crimini—firm and brown and delicious when sautéed.*
- *Enoki—prized by the Japanese for its fragile, long-stemmed form; eaten raw or floated in clear soups.*
- *Morels—wild mushrooms with spongy black heads and thick stems.*
- *Oyster—silky texture and ideal for sautéeing.*
- *Porcini—full-flavored and usually sold dried.*
- *Shiitake—an Asian favorite with dark brown, meaty caps, and an earthy flavor well-suited to stews and soups.*

A caveat: Leave the growing and harvesting of mushrooms to the professionals, for the mushrooms you may encounter in the wild may be poisonous. There is no foolproof way for anyone other than an expert to tell the edible from the deadly.

Corn Pudding

No need to cut fresh corn off the cob for this recipe. Simply combine canned niblet corn with cheese, eggs, and cream to create a memorable accompaniment.

1 can (16 ounces) niblet corn, drained
3/4 cup (3 ounces) shredded Cheddar cheese
1/4 cup thinly sliced fresh basil
6 large eggs
1 1/2 cups heavy cream
1/2 teaspoon salt
1/2 teaspoon hot sauce

1. Preheat the oven to 350°. Butter the inside of a 1 1/2-quart baking dish.
2. In the baking dish, combine the corn, cheese, and basil.
3. In a bowl, combine the eggs, cream, salt, and hot sauce. Pour the egg mixture over the corn mixture.
4. Place the baking dish in a large roasting pan. Add enough hot water to come halfway up the sides of the dish. Bake for 40 to 45 minutes or until the pudding is set and golden.
　　　Yield: 6 servings.

Potato Gratin with Gruyère

A dash of freshly grated nutmeg enhances the sweet, nutty flavor of Gruyère cheese.

4 medium baking potatoes
1 teaspoon salt
1/2 teaspoon dry mustard
1/4 teaspoon ground white pepper
1/4 teaspoon freshly grated nutmeg
1 cup (4 ounces) shredded Gruyère cheese
3/4 cup chicken or vegetable broth
1/2 cup heavy cream
2 tablespoons unsalted butter, cut into bits

1. Preheat the oven to 375°.
2. Peel and thinly slice the potatoes. Pat the slices dry using paper towels.
3. In a small bowl, combine the salt, mustard, white pepper, and nutmeg.
4. In a buttered gratin dish or a shallow baking dish, layer 1/3 of the potatoes, sprinkle with 1/3 of the salt mixture, and top with 1/3 of the cheese. Continue layering the potatoes, salt mixture, and cheese in the same manner, except for the top layer of cheese.
5. Combine the chicken broth and cream. Pour the mixture over the potatoes, top with the remaining 1/3 of the cheese, and dot with the butter. Cover and bake for 45 minutes. Uncover and bake for 20 to 30 minutes more or until the potatoes are tender and the top is golden brown. Let stand for 10 minutes before serving.
　　　Yield: 6 servings.

Braised Red Cabbage, Apples, and Raisins

Pair this sweet-and-savory side with simple meats and poultry such as roast pork or baked chicken.

1/2 cup unsalted butter
1 small onion, minced
1 (2-pound) red cabbage, cored and thinly sliced
1/2 cup golden raisins
Salt and pepper to taste
1 cup port wine
2 McIntosh apples, peeled, cored, and cubed
1/2 cup firmly packed light brown sugar
1/2 teaspoon freshly grated nutmeg

In a large saucepan over medium heat, melt the butter. Add the onion and cook, stirring occasionally, until softened. Add the cabbage, raisins, salt, and pepper and cook, stirring occasionally, for 10 minutes. Add the port and simmer, stirring occasionally, for 15 minutes. Add the apples, brown sugar, and nutmeg and simmer for 5 to 10 minutes, stirring occasionally, or until the cabbage is tender.
　　　Yield: 6 servings.

Corn Pudding

Crabapple, Ham, and Cornbread Dressing

5 tablespoons unsalted butter
1/2 pound country ham, cut into thin strips
1 cup minced onion
2 teaspoons each minced fresh thyme and sage
20 crabapples, peeled, cored, and diced
2 celery stalks, minced
1 sweet red pepper, seeded and minced
5 cups coarsely crumbled cornbread
1/2 cup Madeira wine
1/4 cup minced fresh parsley
Salt and freshly ground pepper to taste

In a large skillet over medium heat, melt the butter. Add the ham and cook, stirring occasionally, until slightly crisp. Add the onion, herbs, crabapples, celery, and sweet red pepper. Cook, stirring occasionally, until the onion is translucent. Transfer the mixture to a large bowl and let cool slightly. Add the cornbread, Madeira, parsley, salt, and pepper. Stir to combine.

Yield: about 10 cups.

Julienne Vegetables with Wild Garlic

4 carrots, peeled
4 celery stalks
4 small zucchini
1 sweet red pepper, seeded
1 sweet yellow pepper, seeded
1 green pepper, seeded
1 bunch scallions, trimmed
1/4 cup olive oil
2 tablespoons minced wild garlic or regular garlic
Salt and freshly ground pepper to taste

1. Cut the vegetables into julienne strips, 2" in length, about 1/4" thick. Set aside.
2. In a large skillet, heat oil over medium-high heat. Add the garlic and cook for 30 seconds, stirring constantly.
3. Add the carrot and cook, stirring, for 1 minute.
4. Add the remaining vegetables and salt and pepper. Cook, stirring, for 6 to 8 minutes more or until the vegetables are crisp-tender.

Yield: 8 servings.

Sweet Potato Soufflé

6 large sweet potatoes (about 5 1/2 pounds), peeled and diced
10 large eggs, separated
1/2 cup firmly packed light brown sugar
1/4 cup honey
1/4 cup unsalted butter, softened
1 teaspoon ground cinnamon
1/4 teaspoon freshly grated nutmeg
Salt and freshly ground pepper to taste
2 vanilla beans, split lengthwise and seeds removed
1/2 cup granulated sugar
Persimmon Glaze, if desired (recipe on opposite page)
1 cup Barbecue Spiced Pecans, if desired (recipe on opposite page)

1. Preheat the oven to 350°.
2. Place the sweet potatoes in a large saucepan. Add salted water to cover. Bring to a boil over high heat. Reduce heat and simmer, covered, for 20 minutes or until tender. Drain and transfer to a bowl.
3. Add the egg yolks, brown sugar, honey, butter, cinnamon, nutmeg, salt, and pepper. Beat until blended well.
4. In a bowl, using an electric mixer, combine the egg whites and vanilla bean seeds. Beat until the whites form soft peaks. Add the sugar, a little at a time, and beat until stiff peaks form.
5. Stir 1/4 of the beaten whites into the sweet potato mixture, then gently fold in the remaining whites.
6. Transfer the mixture to a buttered 13" x 9" baking pan and bake for 1 hour. Top with the Persimmon Glaze and Barbecue Spiced Pecans, if desired.

Yield: 6 to 8 servings.

Persimmon Glaze

¼ cup sugar
6 ripe persimmons, quartered
4 whole cloves
1 (3") cinnamon stick

1. In a saucepan over medium-high heat, combine all the ingredients. Cook, stirring frequently, until the mixture is soft. Continue to simmer, stirring, until the mixture is thick enough to coat the back of a spoon.
2. Discard the cinnamon stick and cloves. Transfer the mixture to a food processor or blender and process until smooth. Strain the mixture through a sieve into a bowl.
Yield: 1 cup.

Barbecue Spiced Pecans

1 pound pecan halves
¼ cup butter, melted
¼ cup firmly packed light brown sugar
¼ teaspoon celery salt
¼ teaspoon paprika
¼ teaspoon dry mustard
A large pinch of cloves
Salt to taste

1. Preheat the oven to 350°.
2. Spread the pecan halves on a baking sheet. Bake the pecans for 10 minutes or until lightly brown and crisp.
3. Transfer the pecans to a bowl. While the pecans are hot, toss with butter.
4. In a small bowl, combine the remaining ingredients. Add the mixture to the pecans and toss to coat. Let cool. Keep leftover pecans in an airtight container for up to 2 weeks.
Yield: about 4 cups.

Candied Yams and Squash

Candied Yams and Squash

4 large yams, unpeeled
2 (1½-pound) acorn or butternut squash
2 cups light corn syrup
2 cups honey or 1 cup honey combined with 1 cup pure maple syrup
1 cup unsalted butter
½ pound light brown sugar
1 teaspoon ground cinnamon
½ teaspoon ground ginger
½ cup dry plain bread crumbs
2 tablespoons bourbon
2 teaspoons vanilla extract

1. Place the yams in a large saucepan. Add water to cover. Bring to a boil and simmer for 25 to 30 minutes or until tender. Drain the yams and let cool to the touch. Peel the yams and cut in half. Set aside.
2. Quarter each squash and remove the seeds. Set aside.
3. In a saucepan, combine the corn syrup, honey, butter, brown sugar, cinnamon, and ginger. Bring to a boil, stirring, and cook over medium-low heat, stirring occasionally, for 30 minutes. Stir in the bread crumbs, bourbon, and vanilla.
4. Preheat the oven to 350°.
5. Arrange the yams and squash in a large buttered baking dish. Pour the syrup mixture over the vegetable mixture and bake for 45 minutes, basting frequently, or until the squash is tender and glazed.
Yield: 8 to 10 servings.

Cranberry, Pomegranate, and Shallot Relish

Roasting shallots mellows their onion flavor and releases their natural sweetness, allowing for a subtle blend of distinctive flavors in this condiment.

8 shallots, unpeeled
1 tablespoon olive oil
Seeds from 6 pomegranates
Juice from 1 orange
Grated zest from 1 orange
1 cup firmly packed light
    brown sugar
2 (3") cinnamon sticks
1 cup port wine
1 pound fresh cranberries

1. Preheat the oven to 375°.
2. In a shallow baking dish, toss the shallots with the oil. Bake, covered, for 30 to 40 minutes or until the shallots are soft. Transfer the shallots to a bowl and let cool. Peel, slice, and set aside the shallots.
3. In a large saucepan over medium heat, combine the pomegranate seeds and orange juice. Bring to a boil, stirring, and simmer until the juice is rendered. Strain the juice through a fine sieve into a saucepan.
4. Add the orange zest, brown sugar, cinnamon sticks, and port to the saucepan. Set the saucepan over medium heat, bring the mixture to a boil, stirring, and simmer, stirring occasionally, for 5 minutes. Add the shallots and cranberries and simmer, stirring, until the cranberries burst. Transfer to a serving dish and serve warm or chilled.
    Yield: about 4 cups.

Orange-Glazed Brussels Sprouts

Fresh sprouts are ideal, but if they're unavailable, substitute two ten-ounce packages of frozen Brussels sprouts and follow the cooking directions on the package.

2 pounds fresh Brussels sprouts
1/4 cup unsalted butter
1/2 cup orange marmalade
2 teaspoons sugar
1/2 teaspoon salt

1. In a large saucepan, combine the sprouts and enough water to cover. Bring to a boil. Reduce heat. Cover and simmer for 10 to 12 minutes or until tender. Drain. Transfer to a serving bowl, and keep warm.
2. In the same saucepan, melt the butter over medium heat. Stir in the marmalade, sugar, and salt. Continue cooking, stirring until hot and blended.
3. Pour the hot sauce mixture over the sprouts in a serving bowl. Toss gently.
    Yield: 6 to 8 servings.

Herb-Roasted New Potatoes

3 pounds small new potatoes,
    unpeeled (about 42 potatoes)
1/2 cup olive oil
1 tablespoon chopped fresh
    rosemary or 1 teaspoon
    dried rosemary
1 tablespoon chopped fresh thyme
    or 1 teaspoon dried thyme
1 tablespoon chopped fresh parsley
Salt and pepper to taste

1. Preheat the oven to 375°. Coat the potatoes with the oil. Arrange the potatoes in a single layer in a 13" x 9" x 2" baking dish. Drizzle any remaining oil over the potatoes.
2. Sprinkle the potatoes evenly with the rosemary, thyme, parsley, salt, and pepper.
3. Bake at 375° for 35 to 55 minutes, depending on the size of the potatoes, or until the potatoes are tender. Turn the potatoes occasionally during baking.
    Yield: 6 to 8 servings.

Herbed Focaccia

Sponge:
1/4 cup warm water (105°F to 115°F)
Pinch of sugar
1 package active dry yeast
1/2 cup minced yellow onion
1 1/2 tablespoons olive oil
2 tablespoons chopped fresh basil
1 1/2 teaspoons chopped fresh
    thyme
1 teaspoon chopped fresh
    rosemary
1/2 teaspoon chopped fresh sage
Freshly ground pepper to taste
1/2 cup warm milk (105°F to 115°F)
1/2 cup plus 2 tablespoons warm
    water (105°F to 115°F)
1 1/2 teaspoons sugar
2 cups all-purpose flour
2 tablespoons chopped, pitted
    calamata olives, if desired

Dough:
1 1/2 teaspoons salt
1 1/2 to 2 cups bread flour

Topping:

1 cup thin strips yellow onion
1½ tablespoons olive oil
1 teaspoon chopped fresh thyme
1 teaspoon chopped fresh rosemary
Freshly ground black pepper
    to taste
¼ cup plain cornmeal
Freshly ground black pepper and
    coarse salt to taste

To make Sponge:

1. Butter a 4-quart bowl. Brush a 12" x 7½" x 2" baking dish with olive oil. Set aside.
2. In a small bowl, combine the ¼ cup warm water and pinch of sugar. Sprinkle the yeast over the water mixture. Let stand 5 minutes.
3. In a small skillet, sauté the minced onion in the hot olive oil over medium heat until soft. Stir in the basil, thyme, rosemary, sage, and pepper. Cook, stirring gently, for 1 minute. Pour the mixture into the buttered bowl.
4. Stir in the warm milk, ½ cup plus 2 tablespoons warm water, 1½ teaspoons sugar, and yeast mixture. Add the 2 cups of flour. Beat at high speed of an electric mixer for 3 minutes. Stir in the olives, if desired.
5. Cover and let rise in warm place (85°) until doubled, about 30 minutes.

To make Dough:

1. Brush a 4-quart bowl with olive oil. Stir the salt into the sponge mixture. Stir in enough of the bread flour with a wooden spoon until the dough forms a ball.
2. Turn the dough out onto a well-floured surface. Knead until smooth and elastic, about 8 to 10 minutes,

Herbed Focaccia

adding enough of the remaining bread flour to keep the dough from sticking.
3. Place the dough in the oiled bowl, turning once to oil the surface. Cover and let rise in a warm place until doubled, about 45 minutes.

To make Topping:

1. In a small skillet, sauté the onion strips in the hot olive oil over medium heat until soft.
2. Add the thyme, rosemary, and pepper. Cook, stirring, for 1 minute. Remove from heat and set aside.

To Assemble:

1. Sprinkle 2 tablespoons of the cornmeal in the prepared baking dish, tilting to coat. Do not shake out the excess cornmeal. Turn the dough into the center of the baking dish. Sprinkle the remaining corn-

meal evenly over the dough.
2. Gently push the dough out from the center toward the sides of the dish, pulling carefully at the ends of the dough to fill all the corners of the baking dish. The dough should fill the dish evenly. Brush the top of the dough with olive oil. Lightly prick the dough at 1" intervals with a fork.
3. Spoon the onion topping over the dough, spreading to within 1" of the edge of the dough. Sprinkle with the pepper and salt.
4. Let rise, uncovered, in a warm place until doubled, about 45 minutes. Preheat the oven to 425°.
5. Bake for 30 minutes. Run a knife around the edge of the dish to loosen the bread. Using 2 spatulas, remove the bread from the dish. Cool on a wire rack. Cut into squares to serve.

Yield: 12 servings.

Skillet Cornbread

For a crispy crust, heat the butter and shortening in the skillets until very hot.

The cornbread batter should sizzle when poured into the hot skillet. The cornbread shown at left was baked in an old-fashioned cast-iron muffin pan.

Cornbread Mix:
4 cups plain cornmeal
4 cups sifted all-purpose flour
1/2 cup sugar
1/3 cup baking powder
2 teaspoons salt, or to taste
1 teaspoon baking soda

Batter:
4 to 6 tablespoons shortening, or
    to taste
4 to 6 tablespoons unsalted
    butter, or to taste
1 1/4 cups buttermilk
1 tablespoon blackstrap molasses,
    or to taste
2 jumbo eggs, beaten lightly

To make Cornbread Mix:
Into a bowl, sift together the cornmeal, flour, sugar, baking powder, salt, and baking soda.

To make Batter:
1. Preheat the oven to 425°.
2. Divide the shortening and butter evenly between 2 (9") cast-iron skillets or 2 (9") dark metal round cake pans. Place skillets in oven until very hot.
3. In a bowl, combine 3 cups of the cornbread mix, buttermilk, molasses, and eggs until just blended.

4. Divide the batter evenly between the skillets. Bake for 15 to 20 minutes or until golden and a cake tester or wooden pick inserted in the center comes out clean.

Yield: two 9" loaves cornbread.

Sweet Potato Crescent Rolls

2 packages active dry yeast
1 cup warm water (105°F to 115°F)
1 cup cooked mashed sweet potato
    (about 3/4 pound uncooked)
1/2 cup sugar
1/2 cup shortening
1 1/2 teaspoons salt
1 large egg, beaten lightly
5 to 5 1/2 cups all-purpose flour
1/4 cup butter, melted

1. In the warmed bowl of an electric mixer, combine the yeast and water. Let stand for 5 minutes.
2. Add the sweet potato, sugar, shortening, salt, and egg. Beat well.
3. Beat in the flour, a little at a time, until a soft dough is formed. Knead the dough in the mixer or by hand for 4 to 5 minutes or until smooth.
4. Transfer the dough to an oiled bowl, turn to coat with the oil, and let rise, in a warm place (85°F), covered with a towel for 1 hour, or until doubled.
5. Punch down the dough and divide into thirds. Roll each third into a 12" circle. Cut each circle into 12 wedges. Brush the dough with the melted butter.

6. Beginning with the wide end, roll up each wedge, tucking the tip under the roll and gently bending it into a curve. Place the rolls on greased baking sheets. Loosely cover with a dish towel and let rise 40 minutes.
7. Preheat the oven to 375°. Bake the rolls for 12 to 15 minutes or until they sound hollow when the bottoms are tapped. Transfer the rolls to wire racks to cool. Store in airtight containers.

Yield: 3 dozen rolls.

Sweet Potatoes

Native to America, sweet potatoes have been growing in the southern states since as early as 1648. This elongated root vegetable has a vivid orange color and a soft, moist consistency when cooked. Its natural sweet flavor pairs well with many accompaniments, such as pecans, dark sugars, bourbon, and syrups.

Select firm, smooth-skinned sweet potatoes, avoiding those with soft spots, bruises, or other signs of decay. Store sweet potatoes in a dry, well-ventilated space, and use them within a couple of weeks. Avoid refrigerating uncooked sweet potatoes, for cold temperatures can cause them to spoil.

Skillet Cornbread

Deep-Dish Black Plum Pie

Pools of satiny custard cradle ruby-colored wedges of fruit pie in this sweet after-dinner delight.

Pie Crust:

3 cups all-purpose flour

1½ teaspoons salt

1 cup cold shortening, cut into bits

3 tablespoons cold butter, cut into bits

¼ cup ice water, or more if needed

Filling:

8 cups thickly sliced black plums (about 15 plums)

1½ cups sugar

¼ cup all-purpose flour

¼ cup cornstarch

1 large egg

1 teaspoon water

Wild Pear Anglaise as an accompaniment, if desired (recipe on opposite page)

To make Pie Crust:

1. Preheat the oven to 450°.

2. Into a bowl, sift together the flour and salt. Add the shortening and butter, and using a pastry blender, work the mixture until the butter is the size of small peas. Add the ¼ cup cold water and toss the mixture until moistened, adding more water if necessary. Form the dough into a ball, pat into a 6" circle, and chill, wrapped in plastic wrap, for 30 minutes.

Deep-Dish Black Plum Pie with Wild Pear Anglaise

To make Filling:

1. In a large saucepan over medium heat, combine the plums, sugar, flour, and cornstarch. Bring to a boil, stirring. Simmer until the sugar melts and the mixture is slightly thickened. Transfer the filling to a bowl and let cool.

2. Roll out ⅔ of the dough into a circle about ⅛" thick and fit onto bottom and up sides of a 9" springform pan. Chill the dough for 30 minutes. Roll out the remaining dough to a ⅛" thickness, and with a pastry wheel, cut it into ½" strips. Arrange strips on a baking sheet and chill.

3. Line the pastry in the springform pan with waxed paper, weight it with dried beans or uncooked rice, and bake for 10 minutes. Remove the paper and weights and bake for 5 minutes more. Pour the filling into the pastry shell.

4. Combine the egg and water. Brush the edges of the pastry shell with the egg mixture and arrange the pastry strips in a lattice pattern over the filling. Brush the strips with the egg mixture and bake for 30 to 35 minutes or until golden brown and bubbling. Let cool to warm, remove

the sides of pan, and transfer pie to a serving plate. Serve with Wild Pear Anglaise, if desired.

Yield: one 9" pie.

Wild Pear Anglaise

Pears:

4 firm baking pears, peeled, cored, and halved

1/2 cup firmly packed light brown sugar

1/2 teaspoon ground cinnamon, or to taste

1/4 teaspoon freshly grated nutmeg, or to taste

2 tablespoons unsalted butter, cut into bits

Custard:

2 cups scalded milk

1/3 cup sugar

1/8 teaspoon salt

6 egg yolks, beaten lightly

To bake Pears:

1. Preheat the oven to 400°.

2. Arrange the pears in a buttered baking dish and sprinkle with the brown sugar, cinnamon, and nutmeg. Dot each pear evenly with the butter. Bake, covered, for 30 to 45 minutes or until the pears are very tender. Transfer the pears and their liquid to a processor or blender and puree until smooth. Transfer the puree to a bowl to cool.

To make Custard:

In the top of a double boiler set over simmering water, combine the milk, sugar, salt, and egg yolks. Cook, stirring, until the mixture is thick enough to coat the back of a spoon.

Stir in the pear puree and cook, stirring, until heated through. Serve with the Deep-Dish Black Plum Pie.

Yield: about 5 cups.

Sour Cream–Pumpkin Pie

Pie Crust:

2 cups all-purpose flour

1/2 teaspoon salt

3/4 cup margarine

5 tablespoons ice water, or more if needed

Filling:

1 cup firmly packed dark brown sugar

1 tablespoon all-purpose flour

1 teaspoon ground cinnamon

1/2 teaspoon each salt, ground ginger, and ground nutmeg

1/4 teaspoon ground cloves

1 cup pureed fresh pumpkin

1 cup evaporated milk

1/2 cup sour cream

2 large eggs, beaten lightly

Topping:

1/4 cup chopped pecans

1/4 cup firmly packed dark brown sugar

1 tablespoon unsalted butter

To make Pie Crust:

1. With a pastry blender or fingertips, combine the flour and salt with the margarine until the mixture resembles coarse meal. Add the water and toss to moisten the dry ingredients. Form the

mixture into a ball; then divide the ball in half. Chill the dough, wrapped in plastic wrap, for 30 minutes.

2. For one 9" pie crust: On a lightly floured surface roll one of the balls of dough into a 1/8" thick circle and fit it into a 9" pie pan, crimping the edge decoratively.

3. Gather any remaining bits of pastry, form them into a ball, and roll to 1/8" thick. With decorative cutters, stamp out desired shapes. Chill the cut-outs until ready to use. Chill the remaining pie dough in plastic wrap for up to 2 days or freeze for up to 1 month.

To make Filling:

1. Preheat the oven to 400°.

2. In a bowl, stir together the brown sugar, flour, cinnamon, salt, and other spices.

3. In another bowl, combine the pumpkin puree, evaporated milk, sour cream, and eggs. Add the dry ingredients to the liquid ingredients and beat until smooth.

4. Pour the filling into the pie crust and bake for 50 to 60 minutes or until set. Arrange the decorative pastry cut-outs on a baking sheet and bake during the last 8 to 10 minutes or until pale golden.

To make Topping:

In a small bowl, combine the pecans, brown sugar, and butter. Sprinkle the mixture over the pie and bake for 5 minutes more or until the butter melts. Top the finished pie with the decorative pastry cut-outs.

Yield: one 9" pie.

HOLIDAY SWEETS

Take the time to bake this year, for as the dough rises and the pudding steams, you will know sweet memories are in the making. From the daintiest cookie to the richest yule log, each sweet treat is a gift of heart and hand.

Cranberry Bread

Cranberry Bread

Fresh cranberries sparkle like crimson jewels in this traditional holiday loaf.

5 cups all-purpose flour

2¹/₂ cups sugar

4 teaspoons baking powder

1¹/₂ teaspoons baking soda

1¹/₄ teaspoons salt

4 large eggs

1¹/₂ cups milk

10 tablespoons unsalted butter, melted

4 teaspoons grated orange zest, or to taste

1 (12-ounce) package fresh cranberries (about 3¹/₂ cups)

2 cups coarsely chopped walnuts

1. Preheat the oven to 350°. Butter 2 (9") loaf pans or similar size decorative molds.

2. In a bowl, sift together the flour, sugar, baking powder, baking soda, and salt.

3. In another bowl, whisk the eggs, milk, butter, and orange zest.

4. Add the liquid ingredients to the dry, stirring until just combined. Fold in the cranberries and walnuts.

5. Divide the mixture between the pans, smoothing the tops, and bake for 50 to 60 minutes or until a cake tester or wooden pick inserted in the center comes out clean. Let cool in the pans on wire racks for 5 minutes. Invert onto wire racks to cool completely.

Yield: 2 loaves.

Apple Strudel

2 tablespoons unsalted butter

2 pounds (about 4 large) Granny Smith apples, peeled, cored, and cubed

¹/₄ cup sugar, or to taste

¹/₂ cup apple juice, divided

1 package unflavored gelatin

¹/₃ cup chopped pecans

¹/₃ cup golden raisins

¹/₂ teaspoon ground cinnamon

4 sheets phyllo dough

Melted butter for brushing the dough

2 tablespoons fresh white bread crumbs or cake crumbs

Sifted confectioners' sugar for dusting

1. Preheat the oven to 450°.

2. In a large skillet or saucepan over medium heat, melt 2 tablespoons butter. Add the apples and sugar and cook, stirring occasionally, until the apples are tender. Transfer to a bowl to cool.

3. In a small, heatproof bowl, combine 2 tablespoons of the apple juice with the gelatin and let stand for 5 minutes. Set the bowl in hot water and stir until the gelatin mixture is dissolved.

4. Add the remaining apple juice and the gelatin mixture to the cooked apples and chill slightly until thickened, stirring occasionally, about 15 minutes. Stir in the pecans, raisins, and cinnamon.

5. Brush 1 sheet of phyllo dough with some of the melted butter; top with a second sheet and brush with the butter. Repeat this procedure until all 4 phyllo sheets are layered and buttered.

6. Sprinkle the bread or cake crumbs on the top phyllo sheet. Spoon the apple mixture onto the top third of the dough, leaving a 2" border at the top and sides. Turn the top border over the apple mixture, fold in the side borders, and roll up the phyllo, jelly-roll fashion.

7. Transfer the strudel to a buttered baking sheet, brush the top and sides with melted butter, and bake for 15 to 20 minutes or until golden. Let cool slightly before cutting. Dust with confectioners' sugar.

Yield: 6 to 8 servings.

Panettone

The tall cylindrical shape of this fruit-studded Italian bread lends a stately air to a brunch buffet.

Sponge:
1 tablespoon active dry yeast
1 cup warm water (105°F to 115°F)
1 cup all-purpose flour

Starter:
1/4 cup unsalted butter, softened
3 tablespoons sugar
2 large eggs
1 to 1 3/4 cups all-purpose flour

Dough:
1/4 cup unsalted butter, softened
1 cup sugar
4 egg yolks
2 large eggs
4 teaspoons honey
2 teaspoons vanilla extract
1/4 teaspoon salt
Grated zest of 2 lemons
Grated zest of 2 oranges
1 cup raisins, plumped in hot
    water and drained
1/2 cup chopped candied citrus peel
2 to 3 cups all-purpose flour

To make Sponge:
In a bowl, combine the yeast and water. Whisk in the flour and let stand, covered, in a warm place for 30 minutes to 1 hour or until bubbly and doubled.

To make Starter:
In a large bowl, using an electric mixer, beat the butter and sugar for 2 minutes. Add the eggs and beat until combined. Add the sponge mixture and the flour,

one cup at a time, beating until a stiff, smooth dough is formed. Transfer to an oiled bowl, turn the dough to coat it with the oil, and cover with plastic wrap. Let rise in a dry, warm place (85°F) for 1 to 2 hours or until doubled.

To make Dough:
1. In a bowl, using an electric mixer, beat the butter and sugar for 2 minutes. Add the egg yolks and eggs; beat until blended. Add the honey, vanilla, salt, and zests and beat until just blended.

2. Add the egg mixture to the starter mixture, beating until smooth. Add the raisins and candied peel and stir to combine. Gradually add enough of the flour to form a dough and knead for 5 to 8 minutes or until the dough is smooth and elastic. Transfer the dough to an oiled bowl, turn it to coat with the oil, and cover with plastic wrap. Let rise in a dry, warm place for 2 to 3 hours or until tripled.

3. Punch down the dough and divide it in half. Cover with a towel and let stand 15 minutes. Form the dough into two large round balls and transfer each to a greased panettone pan (cylindrical mold) or a round paper panettone mold, available at kitchen-supply stores, or a large clean coffee can. Let rise in a dry, warm place, lightly covered, for 1 1/2 to 2 hours or until doubled.

4. Preheat the oven to 400°. Bake the loaves for 10 minutes. Reduce the oven temperature to 350° and bake for 30 to 40 minutes more or until a cake tester or wooden pick inserted in the center comes out clean.

5. Let cool in the pans for 5 minutes and invert onto wire racks to cool.

Yield: 2 loaves.

Nut Coffeecake with Apricot Filling

1²/₃ cups ground hazelnuts

¹/₂ cup coarse zwieback or rusk
    crumbs

2 teaspoons baking powder

3 eggs

³/₄ cup sugar

¹/₂ cup unsalted butter, melted
    and cooled

²/₃ cup apricot jam

Confectioners' sugar for
    garnish

Nut Coffeecake with Apricot Filling

1. Butter an 8" x 1½" layer cake pan. Dust with extra zwieback or rusk crumbs. Set aside. Preheat the oven to 350°.

2. In a small mixing bowl, mix together the ground nuts, crumbs, and baking powder. Set aside.

3. In a small bowl, using an electric mixer, beat the eggs and sugar at high speed until light and fluffy, about 5 minutes.

4. Gradually beat in the cooled butter. Add the crumb mixture in 3 batches, stirring just until blended after each addition. Pour half the batter into the cake pan. Set the remaining batter aside.

5. Bake at 350° for 15 minutes. Remove the cake from the oven. Spoon small mounds of the apricot jam over the top of the cake, spreading evenly. Pour the remaining cake batter over the jam layer. (The pan will seem very full.)

6. Bake for 25 to 30 more minutes or until the cake pulls away from the sides of the pan and the top springs back when lightly touched.

7. Cool in the pan set on a wire rack. Remove the cake from the pan when cool. Place on a serving plate with the top side up. Sift confectioners' sugar over the top of the cake to garnish.

    Yield: 8 servings.

Cherries

Most cherries are deep maroon to almost black—a color range that can mask signs of decay. Check freshness by looking for signs of shriveling, leaking, or puckering of the skin. Wash cherries thoroughly before you use them. To preserve cherries for later use, wash and pit them as soon as they are picked; then pack in quart bags and freeze.

California Fruitcake

Fruit Mixture:
1 cup dark raisins
1/3 cup dried cranberries
1/3 cup chopped dried apricots
2 ounces candied pineapple
   slices, cut into small wedges
   (1/3 cup)
2 ounces candied cherries, halved
   (1/3 cup)
2 ounces candied orange peel,
   diced (1/3 cup)
2 ounces candied lemon peel,
   diced (1/3 cup)
2 ounces candied citron, diced
   (1/3 cup)
1 1/2 ounces coarsely chopped
   crystallized ginger (1/3 cup)
1/2 cup brandy

Batter:
1 1/2 cups all-purpose flour
1 1/2 teaspoons baking powder
1/2 teaspoon baking soda
1 teaspoon ground cinnamon
1/2 teaspoon ground cloves
1/4 teaspoon ground nutmeg
1/4 teaspoon salt
1/2 cup unsalted butter, softened
3/4 cup firmly packed brown sugar
2 eggs
1/2 cup milk
1 cup chopped walnuts
1/2 cup chopped blanched almonds

To make Fruit Mixture:
In a large bowl, combine all of the fruits, ginger, and brandy. Mix well. Cover and let stand for several hours or overnight, stirring occasionally.

To make Batter:
1. Butter 2 (8½" x 4½" x 2½") loaf pans or 4 (6" x 3" x 2") loaf pans. Line the bottoms of the pans with waxed paper. Butter the waxed paper. Set the pans aside. Preheat the oven to 325°.
2. Sift together the flour, baking powder, baking soda, cinnamon, cloves, nutmeg, and salt. Set aside.
3. In a large mixing bowl, using an electric mixer, beat the butter at medium speed until creamy. Gradually add the brown sugar, beating until light and scraping the sides of the bowl often. Add the eggs, one at a time, beating well after each addition.
4. Add the flour mixture alternately with the milk, beating at low speed until blended after each addition. Stir in the fruit mixture and nuts.

5. Spoon the batter into the pans. Pack the batter evenly in the pans, pressing the batter down firmly with the back of a wooden spoon. Arrange the pans on a baking sheet.
6. Bake at 325° for 1 hour for the medium loaves or 40 minutes for the small loaves or until a cake tester or wooden pick inserted in the center comes out clean. Cool in the pans on wire racks for 10 minutes. Run a knife around the edges of the cakes to loosen. Remove from the pans. Peel off the waxed paper. Cool on the wire racks.
7. Wrap the cooled cakes in cheese-cloth soaked in additional brandy. Wrap each cake in aluminum foil. Refrigerate the cakes for at least 1 month, brushing occasionally with more brandy.

Yield: 2 medium or 4 small loaves.

California Fruitcake

Apricot-Almond Bars

Crust:

10 tablespoons cold unsalted
butter, cut into bits

5 tablespoons sugar

2 tablespoons lightly beaten egg

2 cups all-purpose flour

Filling:

2/3 cup sugar

2 tablespoons light corn syrup

1 1/2 tablespoons honey

1 teaspoon lemon juice

1/4 cup heavy cream

1/4 cup milk

1 2/3 cups sliced almonds
(5 ounces)

1 cup chopped dried apricots

1 cup dried sour cherries

To make Crust:

1. In a bowl, using an electric mixer
with the paddle attachment, mix the
butter and sugar on low speed until
combined. Stir in the egg. Add the
flour and mix until combined. Chill the
dough, covered, for 30 minutes or until
firm.

2. Preheat the oven to 350°.

3. Roll out the dough on a lightly
floured surface into a 15" x 12" rec-
tangle and fit it into a 9" x 13" pan.
The dough should come 1" up the
sides of the pan. Place a piece of
parchment paper over the dough,
cover with pie weights or dried
beans, and bake for 15 minutes or
until the edges of the dough are
golden brown. Remove the weights
or beans and paper; then bake the
crust for 5 minutes more. Let cool.

To make Filling:

In a saucepan over medium heat,
combine the sugar, corn syrup,
honey, and lemon juice. Bring the
mixture to a boil, stirring, and simmer for 2 minutes. Remove the pan
from heat and stir in the cream and
milk. Stir in the almonds, apricots,
and cherries. Spread the fruit mixture
over the crust and bake for 15 minutes or until the nuts are lightly gold-
en. Cut the bars while still warm.
(The bars will keep for several days,
but are best eaten the day they are
baked. Store in an airtight container
at room temperature.)

Yield: 12 to 16 bars.

Ginger

*A cornerstone of Christmas,
ginger flavors favorite memories:
gingerbread men with currant
eyes; gingerbread houses frosted
with fluffy icing; and rich, dark
squares of cakelike gingerbread
with tart lemon sauce.*

*For fresh ginger, purchase
the knobby gingerroot whole.
Store it in a paper towel inside a
plastic bag in the refrigerator for
up to three weeks. When ready
to use the ginger, cut off the
largest knobs; then peel the skin
with a vegetable peeler, trying
not to remove too much of the
flavorful flesh just under the skin.*

Snappy Gingersnaps

Fragrant ginger perfumes the air
as these delicately crisp wafers bake
to golden perfection.

1 1/2 cups sugar

1 cup unsalted butter, softened

1/4 cup molasses

1 large egg

2 1/4 cups all-purpose flour

1 1/2 tablespoons grated fresh ginger

4 teaspoons ground ginger

2 teaspoons baking soda

1/4 teaspoon salt

1. Preheat the oven to 350°.

2. In a bowl, using an electric mixer
with the paddle attachment, beat
the sugar and butter at medium
speed until light and creamy. Add
the molasses and egg. Beat until
combined. Decrease speed to low
and add the flour, grated ginger,
ground ginger, baking soda, and
salt, beating until just combined.
Do not overmix.

3. Using 1 tablespoon of dough for
each cookie, roll the dough into 1"
balls and place 2" apart on lightly
greased or parchment-lined baking
sheets. Bake for 12 to 13 minutes or
until flat and evenly browned. Cool
completely before removing the
cookies from the baking sheets.
(The cookies will keep for several
days, though they are best eaten the
day they are baked. Store in an airtight container at room temperature.)

Yield: about 44 cookies.

Apricot-Almond Bars and Snappy Gingersnaps

Espresso Meringues

1 cup plus 2 tablespoons
    confectioners' sugar, sifted
1/3 cup sugar
5 tablespoons instant espresso
    powder
7 large egg whites

1. Preheat the oven to 325°.
2. In a bowl, sift the confectioners'
sugar, sugar, and espresso powder.
3. In a mixing bowl, using an electric
mixer, beat the egg whites at medium
speed until frothy. Increase the speed
to high and gradually add 3 tablespoons of the sugar mixture, beating
until soft peaks form. Gradually add
the remaining sugar mixture and beat
until the whites are stiff and glossy
and the sugar is dissolved.
4. Line the baking sheets with parchment paper or waxed paper. Using a
pastry bag fitted with a star tip, pipe
the meringue into varying shapes
onto the parchment-lined sheets
spacing the meringues 2" apart. Bake
for 1 hour or until the meringues are
dry. Let cool completely in the oven
with the oven door closed for several
hours or overnight. Store in an airtight container at room temperature.

    Yield: about 3 dozen meringues.

Ruby Poached Pears

(photograph on page 13)

6 firm, ripe pears, such as Bosc
    or Anjou
1 (64-ounce) bottle cranberry-
    raspberry juice
1 cup sugar
4 whole cloves
3 bay leaves
Red food coloring to taste
Fresh berries and fresh mint sprigs
    for garnish

1. Peel and core the pears leaving the
stems intact.
2. In a large saucepan, combine the
cranberry-raspberry juice, sugar,
cloves, bay leaves, and food coloring.
Bring the mixture to a boil and
simmer, stirring until the sugar is
dissolved.
3. Add the pears and simmer, covered, turning occasionally for 10 to
12 minutes or until just tender.
Transfer the pears to a serving bowl,
let cool, and chill overnight.
4. Serve the pears garnished with
fresh berries and fresh mint sprigs.

    Yield: 6 ruby pears.

Pears

Pears usually arrive at the market several days shy of their peak. Let pears stand at room temperature for a few days. When the stem end yields to gentle pressure, the flesh will be creamy, soft, and sweet.

    Bartlett, the summer pear, has a peak season in July and August, though it can be found year-round at markets.

    Several types of pears peak in time for the holidays:
• Anjou pears are egg-shaped and bright green with a slight golden glow when ripe.
• Golden brown Bosc pears are among the slowest to ripen. A Bosc's long, tapered neck and spicy flavor make it well-suited for poaching.
• Comice pears, known as Christmas pears, have a bright green skin that blushes to crimson as they ripen.
• Small Seckel pears have olive-green skin that yields to a rosy red-gold as the dense flesh turns mild and sweet.
• Nelis pears have a light brown russeting over green skin, turning golden when ripe. Almost round, the creamy, winey-sweet Nelis is firm enough for canning.

Espresso Meringues

Cherries Jubilee

Cherries Jubilee

2 cups firmly packed dark brown
    sugar
2 pounds fresh Bing cherries or 3
    (17-ounce) cans dark sweet
    cherries, drained
5 whole cloves
Zest of 2 oranges
1 star anise, available at specialty-
    food shops
1 cup brandy
Ice cream and puff pastry rounds
    as accompaniments

1. In a saucepan over medium heat,
combine the sugar, cherries, cloves,
orange zest, and anise. Bring the mixture to a boil, stirring; then simmer,
covered, until the cherries are soft.
2. Pour the brandy over the cherries; do
not stir. Return the mixture to a simmer
and ignite the brandy using a long-
stemmed match. When the flames die
down, spoon the cherry mixture over ice
cream. Top with frozen puff pastry rounds
baked according to package directions.
    Yield: 6 to 8 servings.

Sixpenny Pudding

Pudding:
1½ cups self-rising flour, sifted
1½ cups currants
1½ cups golden raisins
1¼ cups light muscovado sugar,
    or raw sugar
½ cup fresh wholemeal bread
    crumbs
¼ pound suet
1 teaspoon ground ginger
1 teaspoon ground allspice
1 medium egg, beaten lightly
¾ cup milk
Silver coins, double-wrapped in
    squares of waxed paper

Butterscotch Sauce:
½ cup light muscovado sugar, or
    raw sugar
⅔ cup whipping cream
2 tablespoons unsalted butter
1 teaspoon vanilla extract
Crème fraîche for garnish

To make Pudding:
1. In a bowl, combine the flour, currants, raisins, sugar, bread crumbs,
suet, ginger, and allspice.
2. In another bowl, beat the egg and
milk. Add the dry ingredients to the milk
mixture, a little at a time, and stir until
combined well. Stir in the coins.
3. Transfer the mixture to a buttered
6-cup pudding mold or bowl, being
sure the coins are evenly distributed.
4. Cover the mold with the lid or a
double layer of aluminum foil and tie
with string. Set aside.
5. Set a rack in the bottom of a kettle
or stockpot, add enough water to

reach halfway up the side of the mold, and bring the water to a boil. Keep the water at a brisk—but not rolling—boil, covered with the lid of the kettle or pot. Place the mold in the kettle, cover the kettle, and steam the pudding for 2½ to 3 hours, adding more water as it evaporates.

To make Butterscotch Sauce:

1. In a small saucepan, combine all the ingredients and bring to a simmer, stirring. Simmer for 2 to 3 minutes or until the sauce is thick and creamy. Set aside.

2. To serve, remove the mold from the kettle, remove the lid, and let the pudding stand in the mold on a wire rack for 15 minutes. Turn the mold onto its side, rap it gently all around to loosen the pudding, and unmold the pudding carefully onto an ovenproof dish. Pour the Butterscotch Sauce over the top. Place in a 400° oven for 3 to 4 minutes or until piping hot and bubbling. Serve at once with a dollop of crème fraîche on each slice.

Yield: 8 servings.

Hazelnut and Chocolate Tart

Clouds of chocolate sprinkled with fresh strawberries and toasted hazelnuts crown this tempting tart.

Pastry:
1½ cups all-purpose flour
½ cup confectioners' sugar
10 tablespoons unsalted butter, cut into bits
2 tablespoons ground almonds
1 large egg, beaten lightly
1 to 2 tablespoons ice water

Filling:
2 cups heavy cream
1 pound bittersweet chocolate, chopped
1 cup chopped toasted hazelnuts
Strawberries and toasted hazelnuts for garnish

To make Pastry:

1. In a bowl, sift together the flour and sugar. Add the butter and almonds and stir until the mixture resembles coarse meal. Add the egg and enough ice water to make a dough. Form the dough into a ball and chill, wrapped in plastic wrap, for 30 minutes.

2. Preheat the oven to 350°.

3. On a lightly floured surface, roll out the dough into a round ⅛" thick and fit it into a 10" tart pan. Line the dough with a round of waxed paper, weight it with dried beans or uncooked rice, and bake for 20 minutes. Remove the paper and weights and bake the dough for 5 to 10 minutes more or until golden. Transfer to a wire rack to cool.

To make Filling:

1. In a saucepan over medium heat, bring the cream to a boil. Remove from heat, add the chocolate, and stir the mixture until smooth. Transfer 1½ cups of the chocolate mixture to a bowl and reserve. Stir the hazelnuts into the remaining chocolate mixture. Pour into the pastry shell and chill.

2. Chill the reserved chocolate mixture until firm; then transfer the mixture to a pastry bag fitted with a star tip. Pipe the chocolate mixture onto the tart in a decorative pattern and chill for 2 hours or until firm. Before serving, garnish the tart with the strawberries and hazelnuts and let stand 10 minutes to soften.

Yield: one 10" tart.

Hazelnuts

Hazelnuts are also called filberts in honor of France's St. Philibert of Burgundy, whose feast fell during the autumn nut harvest.

Hazelnuts grow in clusters close to the stem of the hazel tree. The nuts are harvested in October after nearly nine months of slow growth. After harvest, they are bleached to the lovely light brown color known as hazel. Their rich, distinctive flavor is delightful in cakes and other baked goods, as well as in poultry stuffings.

Pear and Walnut Tart

Select firm pears that yield slightly to gentle pressure for this winter dessert.

6 tablespoons unsalted butter

1 cup sugar

1 cup walnut halves

6 firm Bosc or Bartlett pears, peeled, cored, and quartered

1 (10"-round) puff pastry, rolled ⅛" thick and lightly pricked with a fork

1. Preheat the oven to 400°.
2. In a heavy, ovenproof 10" skillet set over medium heat, melt the butter. Add the sugar, and cook, stirring until the sugar turns golden and begins to caramelize. Stir in the walnuts. Add the pears and turn to coat with the caramel. (The pan will be crowded, but the pears will shrink during cooking.)
3. Bake the pear mixture for 30 to 45 minutes or until the pears are tender, depending upon their firmness. Remove from the oven and let cool slightly.
4. Meanwhile, place the puff pastry on a baking sheet and bake for 10 minutes. Turn and bake for 10 to 12 minutes more or until golden brown.
5. To serve: If the pear mixture is very liquid, pour most of the liquid into a bowl. Top the pear mixture with the puff pastry round, invert a serving plate over the top of the skillet, and carefully invert the tart onto the plate. Scrape any remaining fruit or caramel onto the tart and, with a spatula, smooth the tart's surface. Spoon the reserved juices over the tart.
   Yield: 6 to 8 servings.

Apple-Rum Pie

Pie Crust:

1¾ cups all-purpose flour

⅓ cup shortening, cut into small pieces

6 tablespoons unsalted butter, cut into small pieces

3 tablespoons sugar

⅛ teaspoon salt

3 to 4 tablespoons ice water

Filling:

½ cup sugar

1 tablespoon all-purpose flour

2 teaspoons ground cinnamon

½ teaspoon ground nutmeg

2 pounds Granny Smith apples, peeled, cored, and cut in ½"-thick slices (7 cups)

⅓ cup heavy cream

¼ cup dark rum

Egg Wash:

1 egg, beaten lightly

¼ cup cold water

To make Pie Crust:

1. In a food processor, combine the flour, shortening, butter, sugar, and salt. Process until the mixture resembles coarse meal.
2. With the processor running, add the ice water through the feed tube until the dough pulls away from the sides of the bowl and forms a ball.
3. Divide the dough into ⅔ and ⅓ portions. Form each portion into a disk shape. Wrap in plastic wrap and refrigerate for 1 hour.

To make Filling:

1. In a small bowl, combine the sugar, flour, cinnamon, and nutmeg. Stir until blended. Toss with the apple slices in a large bowl.
2. Drizzle the cream and rum over the apple mixture. Toss well.

To assemble:

1. Preheat the oven to 450°. On a heavily floured surface or between sheets of floured waxed paper, roll out ⅔ of the dough to a 12" circle. Line a 9" pie plate with the pastry. (The dough will be sticky and fragile to handle.)
2. Spoon the filling into the pie crust. Roll out the remaining pastry and fit it over the top of the filling. Trim the excess dough. Seal and flute the edges. Cut slits in the top crust to allow steam to escape.
3. In a small bowl, whisk together the egg and cold water. Brush the egg mixture over the pie crust. (There will be egg mixture left over.) Bake pie crust at 450° for 20 minutes.
4. Reduce the oven temperature to 375°. Bake the pie 40 minutes more until the filling is bubbling in the center and the apples are tender. If necessary, tent the pie with aluminum foil toward the end of the baking time to prevent overbrowning.
   Yield: 6 servings.

Apple-Rum Pie

Eggnog Pie with Pecan Crust

Pie Crust:
2½ cups ground pecans (9 ounces pecan pieces)
⅓ cup sugar
¼ cup unsalted butter, melted

Filling:
2 envelopes unflavored gelatin
¼ cup cold water
2 tablespoons brandy
6 egg yolks
½ cup sugar
2 cups scalded milk
¼ cup dark rum
2 teaspoons vanilla extract
1 cup heavy cream

Topping:
1 cup heavy cream
2 tablespoons sifted confectioners' sugar
Chocolate curls and fresh raspberries for garnish

To make Pie Crust:
1. Butter a 10" pie plate. In a medium bowl, combine the pecans, sugar, and butter. Stir well. Press the mixture firmly into the pie plate. Cover and refrigerate for 30 minutes.
2. Preheat the oven to 375°. Bake the crust at 375° for 15 minutes or until lightly browned. Cool on a wire rack.

To make Filling:
1. In a small bowl, sprinkle the gelatin over the cold water and brandy. Let stand for 10 minutes.

2. In a small mixing bowl, using an electric mixer, beat the egg yolks and sugar at high speed until the mixture forms ribbons when the beaters are lifted, about 5 minutes. Pour the mixture into a large, heavy saucepan.
3. Slowly stir in the scalded milk. Cook over medium-low heat, stirring constantly, until the mixture thickens enough to coat the spoon and a thermometer registers 172°. Do not boil. Remove from heat.
4. Stir in the gelatin mixture until dissolved. Stir in the rum and vanilla.
5. Pour the custard mixture into a medium bowl set in a larger bowl of ice and cold water. Cool, stirring often, for 15 to 20 minutes or until the filling just starts to set around the edges. Remove the bowl from the ice water bath at once. (Watch carefully. Do not let the filling set.) Set aside.
6. Working quickly, in a chilled medium bowl, beat 1 cup cream to soft peaks. Gradually fold into the custard mixture. (If necessary, refrigerate the filling a few minutes until it mounds when spooned.)
7. Spoon the filling into the cooled crust. Refrigerate for 1 hour or until set.

To make Topping:
1. In a chilled medium bowl, beat the remaining 1 cup cream with the confectioners' sugar until the mixture forms stiff peaks.
2. Garnish the pie with the whipped-cream topping, chocolate curls, and raspberries.

Yield: 8 servings.

Eggnog Pie with Pecan Crust

Vanilla

Vanilla comes from the fruit of an orchid that blooms for just a few hours only once a year on vines that grow up to fifty feet. Each blossom produces a single bean that must be cured to develop its distinct flavor. The result—a wizened, blackened bean—is prized for the tiny, edible seeds inside.

Most cooks use vanilla extract, a convenient way to impart vanilla's richness. Choose only pure vanilla extract, for imitation vanilla is not made from vanilla beans and can be harsh and unpleasant.

Some cooks insist on using whole vanilla beans for more intense flavor. Slit the bean lengthwise; then steep it in hot liquid to release its flavor. Beans used this way can be reused several times. Rinse and dry the bean; then wrap it in plastic wrap and refrigerate it in a sealed jar. When the bean loses its scent, it is time to replace it.

For the most pronounced vanilla flavor, scrape the seeds from inside the bean directly into the cooking liquid. The scrapings from a whole bean are equivalent to 1½ to 2 tablespoons of vanilla extract.

Cassis Mousse Cake

(photograph on page 120)

Cassis Mousse:

11 ounces cassis puree, made by pureeing 1 pint of black currants or a similar berry until smooth

²/₃ cup sugar

1½ cups heavy cream, divided

4 teaspoons unflavored gelatin

1 (9") Génoise (Sponge Cake) (recipe below, right)

1 (3-ounce) package ladyfingers, split

Glaze:

1 cup apricot preserves, sieved

⅓ cup reserved cassis puree

To make Cassis Mousse:

1. In a saucepan over medium heat, combine the puree and sugar and cook, stirring until the sugar is melted. Press the mixture through a sieve into a bowl and chill.

2. In a small, heatproof bowl, combine ⅓ cup heavy cream with the gelatin and let stand for 5 minutes. Set the bowl in a pan of hot water and stir until the mixture is smooth. Stir the gelatin mixture into the chilled cassis puree. Reserve ⅓ cup of the puree mixture for the glaze. In a bowl, using an electric mixer, beat the remaining cream until it forms soft peaks. Gradually add all but the reserved ⅓ cup puree mixture to the cream mixture and fold together gently. Chill, covered, until ready to use.

3. Cut the sponge cake into 2

Cassis Mousse Cake

(½"-thick) layers. Arrange 1 cake layer in the bottom of a 9" springform pan and line the sides of the pan with the ladyfingers. Add a 1" layer of the chilled mousse. Top the mousse layer with the second cake layer. Add another layer of mousse. Chill until ready to glaze.

To make Glaze:

In a small saucepan over medium heat, melt the apricot preserves, simmering until lightly thickened. Stir in the reserved puree mixture. Let cool for 5 minutes and spoon over the top of the cake. Chill until ready to serve.

Yield: 8 to 10 servings.

Génoise (Sponge Cake)

3 large eggs

½ cup sugar

1 teaspoon vanilla extract

3 tablespoons butter, melted and cooled

½ cup all-purpose flour

1. Preheat the oven to 350°. Butter a 9" cake pan. Line the pan with parchment paper or waxed paper; butter and flour the paper, shaking out the excess flour.

2. In a bowl, using an electric mixer, beat the eggs. Add the sugar, a little at a time, and beat for 4 minutes or until the mixture is thick enough to form a ribbon when the beater is lifted. Add the vanilla and beat until combined.

3. In a small bowl, combine 1 cup of the sugar mixture and the butter. Fold until combined.

4. Sift the flour over the sugar mixture, ⅓ at a time, folding the flour in after each addition. Add the butter mixture and fold until combined.

5. Pour the batter into the prepared pan, smoothing the top into an even layer. Bake for 15 to 20 minutes or until a cake tester or wooden pick inserted in the center comes out clean. Let the cake cool in the pan for 5 minutes. Invert the cake onto a wire rack and let cool completely.

   Yield: one 9" sponge cake.

Mocha Yule Log

(photograph on page 120)

Cake:

5 large eggs, separated
½ cup plus 2 tablespoons sugar, divided
1 teaspoon vanilla extract
¾ cup all-purpose flour
⅛ teaspoon salt

Buttercream:

1 cup milk
4 egg yolks
⅔ cup sugar
6 ounces semisweet chocolate, chopped into bits
¼ cup hot water
2 tablespoons instant espresso powder
1½ cups cold unsalted butter, cut into bits and softened
Meringue mushrooms and chocolate leaves for garnish, if desired

To make Cake:

1. Preheat the oven to 350°.

2. Butter a 15" jelly-roll pan and line with parchment paper, leaving a 2" overhang on each of the short ends. Butter the paper and dust with flour, shaking out the excess.

3. In a large bowl, using an electric mixer, beat the 5 egg yolks until combined. Gradually add ½ cup of the sugar and beat until the mixture is thick and forms a ribbon when the beaters are lifted, about 5 minutes. Beat in the vanilla.

4. In another bowl, using an electric mixer, beat the 5 egg whites until they form soft peaks. Add the remaining 2 tablespoons of sugar, one at a time, and beat until they form firm peaks. Gently fold the whites into the batter. Sift together the flour and the salt. Sift the mixture over the batter, ⅓ at a time, and fold in each addition until the batter is smooth.

5. Pour the batter into the prepared pan, spreading evenly. Bake the cake for 15 minutes, or until it pulls away from the sides of the pan and a cake tester or wooden pick inserted in the center comes out clean. Let the cake cool slightly. Pull the edges of the paper away from the pan, and cover the cake with another piece of parchment paper and a baking sheet. Invert the cake onto the baking sheet. Carefully peel off the paper from the bottom of the cake, and cover the cake with a clean piece of parchment paper and a large wire rack. Invert the cake onto the rack so that it is right side up. Let cool to room temperature. Roll the cake up lengthwise in the paper and let cool completely.

To make Buttercream:

1. In a saucepan over medium heat, cook the milk just until bubbles begin to form around the edge. In a bowl, whisk together the egg yolks and sugar. Gradually whisk in the milk and return the milk mixture to the saucepan. Cook the mixture over medium-low heat, stirring, until the mixture is thick enough to coat the back of a spoon. Do not boil. Remove from heat. Add the chocolate, and stir until smooth.

2. Combine the hot water and espresso powder. Add the espresso mixture to the custard mixture and stir until smooth. Let the mixture cool to room temperature. Using an electric mixer, gradually beat in the butter until the mixture is light and fluffy.

3. Unroll the cake and spread some of the buttercream filling evenly over the cake, leaving a 1" border on each of the long sides. Roll up the cake lengthwise.

4. Cut a 2"-thick piece diagonally from each end of the cake and set the pieces aside. Transfer the cake to a serving tray and arrange the reserved end pieces on top of the cake to simulate sawed-off branches. Spread the buttercream over the top and sides of the cake. Gently pull the tines of a fork lengthwise over the buttercream to simulate bark. Garnish with meringue mushrooms and chocolate leaves, if desired. Chill until ready to serve. Let the cake come to room temperature before serving.

   Yield: 8 to 10 servings.

Resources

BAKING SUPPLIES & SPECIALTY FOODS

Harry and David Co.
2518 South Pacific Highway
Medford, OR 97501
www.harryanddavid.com
(800) 547-3033

New York Cake & Baking Distributor
56 West 22nd Street
New York, NY 10010
(800) 942-2539
$5 for catalog

CANDLES

Pourette Candle Making Supply
1418 Northwest 53rd Street
P.O. Box 17056
Seattle, WA 98107-0756
(206) 789-3188
Free introductory catalog

Primavera, Inc.
312 Michigan Avenue
Decatur, GA 30030
(404) 373-3914

DECORATIVE PAPERS & WRAPPING SUPPLIES

Caspari
225 Fifth Avenue, #637
New York, NY 10010
(800) CASPARI

The Flower Market
345 West Manhattan Avenue
Santa Fe, NM 87501
(505) 982-9663

Kate's Paperie
561 Broadway
New York, NY 10012
(888) 941-9169
$3 for catalog

Loose Ends
P.O. Box 20310
Keizer, OR 97307
(503) 390-7457
$5 for catalog

Victorian Trading Company
P.O. Box 411341
Kansas City, MO 64141-1341
www.victoriantradingco.com
(800) 718-2380
Free catalog

ESSENTIAL OILS

Lavender Lane
7337 Roseville Road, Suite 1
Sacramento, CA 95842
(916) 334-4400
Free catalog

The Rosemary House
120 South Market Street
Mechanicsburg, PA 17055
(717) 697-5111

FEATURED INNS & SHOPS

Angelina's Tea Parlour
21317 Highway 99 East
P.O. Box 254
Aurora, OR 97002
(503) 678-3303

Anne Fontaine
93 Greene Street
New York, NY 10012
(212) 343-3154 or
318 Boylston Street
Boston, MA 02116
(617) 423-0366 or
La Chemise Blanche
5450 West Lovers Lane, #131
Dallas, TX 75209
(214) 956-0800

Blackberry Farm
1471 West Millers Cove Road
Walland, TN 37886
(423) 984-8166

Fredericksburg Herb Farm
402 Whitney Street
Fredericksburg, TX 78624
(830) 997-8615
www.fredericksburgherb
farm.com

Tante Huppé Inn
424 Jefferson Street
Natchitoches, LA 71457
(318) 352-5342

FLORAL SUPPLIES

The Flower Market
345 West Manhattan Avenue
Santa Fe, NM 87501
(505) 982-9663

Galveston Wreath Company
1124-25th Street
Galveston, TX 77550-4409
(409) 765-8597
Free catalog

Tom Thumb Workshops
P.O. Box 357
Mappsville, VA 23407
(800) 526-6502

FRESH EVERGREENS

Bald Mountain Farm
988 Willet Miller Road
P.O. Box 138
Todd, NC 28684
(888) 611-2129
Free catalog

**Laurel Springs Christmas
  Tree Farm**
7491 Highway 18 South
P.O. Box 85
Laurel Springs, NC 28644
(800) 851-2345
Free catalog

Omni Farm, Inc.
1369 Calloway Gap Road
West Jefferson, NC 28694
www.omnifarm.com
(800) 873-3327
Free catalog

RIBBON

**Just Accents, Inc./
  Impressions**
225 Fifth Avenue, #419
New York, NY 10010
(888) 389-0550
Free catalog

Midori
708 Sixth Avenue North
Seattle, WA 98104
(800) 659-3049

Offray Ribbon Company
360 Route 24
Chester, NJ 07930
www.offray.com
(908) 879-4700

WREATH SUPPLIES

Galveston Wreath Company
1124-25th Street
Galveston, TX 77550-4409
(409) 765-8597
Free catalog

Shrock's International
P.O. Box 538
Bolivar, OH 44612
(330) 874-3700

YARNS

Brown Sheep Company, Inc.
100662 County Road 16
Mitchell, NE 69357
(800) 826-9136

Designer & Recipe Credits

Antrim 1844
Taneytown, Maryland
Eggnog Pie with Pecan Crust,
  page 135

Peggy Barnhart
Page 97 (left)

A.J. Batafarona
Vanilla Milk Punch, page 101;
  Vanilla-Flavored Sugar, page
  101; Vanilla Brandy, page 101

Cesar Benitez
Tart Apple and Squash Soup,
  page 105; Braised Red Cabbage,
  Apples, and Raisins, page 111;
  Skillet Cornbread, page 117

The Berghoff
Chicago, Illinois
Apple Strudel, page 122

Craig Béro
Candied Yams and Squash, page 113

Roscoe Betsill
Potato Gratin with Gruyère,
  page 111

Castle at Tarrytown
Tarrytown, New York
Cassis Mousse Cake, page 136;
  Mocha Yule Log, page 137

Cedar Grove Plantation
Edgefield, South Carolina
Julienne Vegetables with Wild
  Garlic, page 112; Sweet Potato
  Crescent Rolls, page 117

Janice Cox
Pages 79–81

Neil Di Teresa
Page 67 (top)

Christi Finch
Word of Mouth

New York, New York
Corn Pudding, page 111; Sour
  Cream-Pumpkin Pie, page 119;
  Cranberry Bread, page 122

Lauren Groveman
Herbed Focaccia, page 114

Margot Hotchkiss
Page 83

Susan Kochman
New England Catering Company
Cornwall Bridge, Connecticut
Wild Mushroom Bisque, page 105;
  Fruit-Stuffed Crown Roast of
  Pork, page 106; Herb-Roasted
  New Potatoes, page 114; Apple-
  Rum Pie, page 132

Sue Lawrence
Sixpenny Pudding, page 130

Les Airelles
Courchevel, France
Hazelnut and Chocolate Tart,
  page 131

Emily Luchetti
Apricot-Almond Bars, page 126;
  Snappy Gingersnaps, page 126;
  Espresso Meringues, page 129

Rita J. Morrison
Page 45

**Old Chatham Sheepherding
  Company Inn**
Old Chatham, New York
Panettone, page 123

Olde Pink House
Savannah, Georgia
Goose with Gold Rice and
  Chanterelle Stuffing, page 108;
  Crabapple, Ham, and Cornbread
  Dressing, page 112; Sweet Potato
  Soufflé, page 112; Cranberry,
  Pomegranate, and Shallot Relish,

page 114; Deep-Dish Black Plum
  Pie, page 118

Dondra G. Parham
Page 93

Marlene Parrish
California Fruitcake, page 125

Catherine B. Pewitt
Pages 34 (bottom), 74, 76,
  77 (bottom)

River Wildlife
Kohler, Wisconsin
Warm Cranberry Wassail, page 102

Sardy House
Aspen, Colorado
Cherries Jubilee, page 130

Betsy Cooper Scott
Page 83 (ribbon bookmarks)

Simon Pearce Restaurant
Quechee, Vermont
Pear and Walnut Tart, page 132

Steves Homestead
San Antonio, Texas
Champagne Punch, page 101

Carole Sullivan
Pages 37–39

Carole Rutter Tippett
Page 69

Emelie Tolley
Pages 91, 96

Sally Waldrup
Pages 34 (top), 35, 43

Peggy A. Williams
Pages 46–47, 73

Lois Winston
Page 70 (top)

Photography Credits

PHOTOGRAPHERS:

Jim Bathie
Pages 11 (inset), 16, 19 (bottom), 54–59, 73

Richard Brown
Page 25 (inset)

Pierre Chanteau
Page 130

Stephen Cridland
Pages 62, 63

Cheryl Sales Dalton
Pages 17–18

Katrina Deleon
Page 72

Joshua Greene
Page 71 (inset)

Gross & Daley
Pages 2, 10–11, 13–15, 66, 92 (top), 104, 116

Tina Mucci
Page 115

Starr Ockenga
Cover and pages 32, 64, 67

John O'Hagan
Back cover (right) and pages 5–7, 26, 28–31, 34–35, 37–39, 42, 43, 45–47, 49, 50, 52, 53, 69, 70 (top), 74–76, 77 (bottom), 79, 81, 83, 93, 97 (left)

Toshi Otsuki
Back cover (top, left) and pages 3, 8, 21–23, 24–25, 33, 40, 41, 44, 51, 60, 61, 68, 71 (border), 77 (top), 88, 91, 92 (bottom), 95, 96, 97 (right), 99 (inset), 113, 124

Luciana Pampalone
Pages 65, 125

Steven Randazzo
Pages 84–85, 86, 87, 89, 110, 121 (inset), 122

Michael Skott
Page 102

William P. Steele
Back cover (bottom, left) and pages 27, 70 (bottom), 85 (inset), 90, 101, 103, 107, 118, 120, 133, 134, 136, 144

Charles Walton IV
Page 19 (top)

Alan Weintraub
Pages 98, 127, 128

PHOTO STYLISTS:

Kay Clarke
Back cover (right) and pages 26, 28–31, 49, 50, 52, 53

Joetta Moulden
Pages 54–59

Cecile Y. Nierodzinski
Pages 62, 63

Linda Baltzell Wright
Pages 34, 35, 37–39, 42, 43, 45–47, 69, 70 (top), 73, 74–76, 77 (bottom), 79, 81, 83, 93, 97 (left)

Special Thanks

Barbara and Leon Ashford

Carrie Bloom

Gina Frank

David Graff

Susan and Don Huff

Barbara and Ed Randle

Index

Index